Threads of Memory

A MEMOIR OF THE 1920s

Margaret Ott Onerheim

Margaret Ott Onerheim

IOWA STATE UNIVERSITY PRESS / AMES

FOR PAUL, NEIL,
JEAN, KARI, AND LORA

Margaret Ott Onerheim was born in rural Butler County, Iowa, and has been a lifelong resident of the Midwest. For almost twenty-five years, Mrs. Onerheim taught home economics and English in Iowa and Illinois high schools and junior high schools. She now enjoys her retirement in Ottumwa, Iowa, writing, reading, researching genealogy, and "grandmothering."

© 1993 Iowa State University Press, Ames, Iowa 50010
All rights reserved

Authorization to photocopy items for internal or personal use, or the internal or personal use of specific clients, is granted by Iowa State University Press, provided that the base fee of $.10 per copy is paid directly to the Copyright Clearance Center, 27 Congress Street, Salem, MA 01970. For those organizations that have been granted a photocopy license by CCC, a separate system of payments has been arranged. The fee code for users of the Transactional Reporting Service is 0-8138-0902-9/93 $.10.

⊗ Printed on acid-free paper in the United States of America

First edition, 1993

FRONTISPIECE: *Margaret Ott in front of the old family home.*

Library of Congress Cataloging-in-Publication Data

Onerheim, Margaret Ott.
    Threads of memory: a memoir of the 1920s/Margaret Ott Onerheim. — 1st ed.
        p.   cm.
    ISBN 0-8138-0902-9 (acid-free paper)
    1. Iowa — Social life and customs. 2. Onerheim, Margaret Ott — Childhood and youth. I. Title.
F621.054   1993
977.7 — dc20   93-12733

Marion
from
Paul & Carol

Threads of Memory

I·O·W·A
HERITAGE
COLLECTION

CONTENTS

1 • My Childhood Home • 1

2 • Family Life • 53

3 • As Life Appeared to Me • 89

ACKNOWLEDGMENTS

I wish especially to thank Mary C. Allen, whose constant encouragement and advice made this book possible. Also, thanks to my husband, Bernard Onerheim, for his patience and technical assistance.

1

My Childhood Home

It is a time that will not come again.

JAMES HERRIOT

MOVING IN

In the late winter of 1921, when I was three-and-a-half, my family moved to the farm of George Beal, my mother's paternal grandfather. I was somewhat prepared for the move because the week before, Mama, my eight-month-old brother Robert, and I had gone to call on Mama's cousin's wife, Mrs. Ralph Beal, in the house into which we would be moving. It seemed to be a social call, but I noticed that Mama looked speculatively around the rooms. On the way home she talked about the house, as much to herself as to me: "My little desk will fit in the northeast corner of the kitchen. I think my curtains will fit in the front room all right." The only other memory I have of the visit is seeing a child's potty chair in the ditch south of the driveway.

On moving day the air blew in cold as the friends who were helping us carried our furniture out of the house. In spite of a roaring fire Mama kept going in the kitchen stove, the house became chilled. The house got more and more empty, and I could see out the window that men were driving our livestock north toward the new place. I was excited, running from room to room and getting in Mama's way as she cleaned the house for the family who would be moving in. My brother, Harry, a year older than I, was in and out of the house all day, keeping us abreast of the progress of the outside moving and chattering, "I helped Mr. Dailey move the tools in the machine shed, and it was a big job. I'm going to move to the new place with Pa when he drives the car there. When are you going to move, Mama?"

In late afternoon Mama, Robert, and I rode in the bed of the hayrack with the last load of furniture. The wheels of the wagons that had been going back and forth all day mov-

ing our belongings had cut ruts into the ice and dirty snow of
the road, and the bright sun had caused some melting, making it sloppy underfoot. Mama sat in the back of the hayrack,
her feet dangling over the end of the rack, holding her well-
wrapped cut glass creamer and sugar bowl in her lap and
keeping an eye on the basket packed with her other most-
prized dishes, ready to reach out a hand and steady them if
they seemed in danger of being jiggled too much.

Robert, a solemn little fellow, was swathed in blankets
and propped up in our oval wicker clothes basket. His eyes
darted from one to the other of us and to his surroundings as
he struggled to free his arms. I made funny faces for him and
pulled off my mittens to make finger pictures with my hands,
but he was puckering up to cry as the short trip ended. I
looked to see, but the potty chair was gone from the ditch.

Although the trip was less than a quarter of a mile north,
we moved from Butler County to Floyd County, Iowa. It was
also a landmark move for Mama, from the house where she
(and I) had been born, and where she had lived most of her
life. She had told me stories of visiting her grandpa and her
aunts and uncles many times in the house we now were moving into. From overhearing conversations with Papa, I understood that she didn't look forward to living in an older and
less convenient house.

"Maybe we can make a few changes after we've lived
there awhile," Pa consoled her.

One day before the move, while we were eating supper,
Mama said, "I don't know if this stove is worth moving. See
how uneven it baked this bread? Burned on one side and
nearly raw on the other."

"If we need a new one, this would be a good time to get
it," answered Pa. "What would a new one cost? A good
one—it's no use buying anything but the best."

Mama had her answer ready. She brought out the Mont-
gomery Ward catalog and opened it to the page she had
marked.

"Go ahead and order it, if you're sure it's the one you
want," Pa said, after he had read the description and looked

Harry Ott, age four, and Margaret Ott, age 3.
In the background is the house where
Dorotha Beal Ott and Margaret Ott were born.

at the picture. "We'll have it delivered the day we move."

Mama and I saw it for the first time burning brightly when we came into the house on moving day. It was called a "Copper Clad," and it had handsome chrome trim to brighten up the black iron top and sides. She just stood there and looked at it, and I did, too. I liked to act like Mama.

"Well, Dorothy, how does it suit you?" Pa asked her when he came in.

"I'll have no more excuse for burnt bread. Oh, Paul, it's so pretty. I'll always keep it looking nice like this."

I wove my way around the boxes and baskets packed full of things, in and out of the downstairs rooms. These rooms radiated from the kitchen like spokes from the hub of a wheel, an arrangement that fascinates me to this day.

Most of the kitchen things had been hastily unpacked, but one thing was missing. The little gray velveteen bear Grandpa Freem Beal had send me for Christmas from California was not on the desk where it belonged. Mama assured me that it was packed away somewhere and that it would turn up.

We sat down to eat the meal that had been brought to us by friends who knew Mama would be tired after the busy day. Mama, Papa, Harry, and Robert were here with me, and I was content.

In the spring, when it was warm enough to dig, my great-grandfather had a big, gray, cement storage tank erected west of the well. Then a sink with a pump and drain was installed in the kitchen in the narrow space in front of the cellar stairway. A pipe went down through the cellar to the south side, where a hole was chopped into the cement floor for a drain. Tiles carried the water to the ditch south of the driveway.

While the tank was being built, I walked around it one day and saw a big snake sunning itself on the north side of the tank. It was a long time before I could walk that way again without being afraid. Papa said the snake was probably more afraid of me than I was of it, but I didn't see how that could be possible.

In all of its fifty years, the pantry in this house had had curtains covering its open shelves. Mama thought doors would look better and would help keep out the dust.

Grandpa often came out from his home in Greene to see how things were going. He was a tall man with a long beard and blue eyes that looked kindly at me. We didn't talk much because he couldn't hear my voice, and I was too timid to talk loud to him as Aunt Jen did. If he missed part of the conversation, he said, "Eh? What say? What say?" Harry and I went around impudently saying, "What say? What say?" but we never said it where Grandpa could hear us. He wore bib overalls, as he had all his life, but now they were bleached white from so many washings in Aunt Jen's strong soap. One day he said to Papa, "Doffy thinks she'd like doors over the pantry shelves. What do you think of that?" (He called Mama "Doffy" because he had a Maine accent and because a lot of his teeth were missing.)

"Oh, she's willing to wait awhile," Pa replied.

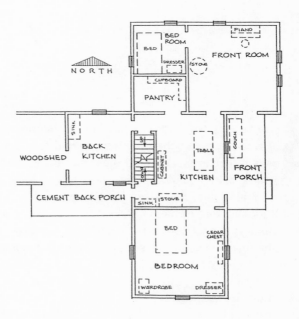

The floor plan of the family home.

"I'd like to see her have what she wants," said Grandpa. "I'll buy the materials if you'll furnish the labor." And that's what happened with this and many other improvements made on the farm until Grandpa's death in 1926.

I remember Papa saying many times, "A fellow couldn't ask for a better landlord. He's a man anyone could do business with."

As the years went by, we settled in and adapted the place to our needs.

This was the home of my childhood.

IMPROVEMENTS

Before spring was over, doors made of the same kind of wood as the kitchen wainscot were fitted over the pantry shelves and painted the same soft gray-blue. "I like that blue color," I told Mama.

"It isn't really blue. It's called 'battleship gray.' "

It still looked blue to me.

As Mama put on fresh shelf paper and unpacked and arranged the dishes that had been in boxes since we moved she sang

> Rings on her fingers,
> Bells on her toes,
> She shall have music wherever she goes,
> For she's Mrs. Mumbo Jumbo Jittaboo Jee.

The fresh paint smell and the pretty flowers on the turned-down edges of the shelf paper made the house feel new.

"It's nice, Mama. I like to live in this house."

With a sigh of relief, Mama exclaimed, "There! That's the last box. I'd begun to think I'd never get those boxes emptied and out of my way."

"But, Mama, where's my little bear? You said we'd find it when we unpacked."

"But we didn't," Mama said firmly.

I couldn't give up hope. I told myself that maybe, just maybe, we would still find it tucked away somewhere. It was like knowing about Santa Claus. If I didn't talk about it, I could still believe.

"We've spent the whole afternoon doing this, and it's time to set the table. We can open these new doors and take the supper dishes to the table. You can help."

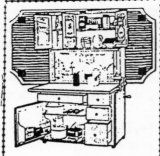

The Hoosier.

The first time it was fun, but it was a long way from cupboard to table to dishpan and back again to the cupboard. The kitchen had an old wooden table but no shelves. We needed a kitchen cabinet.

Mama and I went to Watterson's Furniture Store to look at the cabinets there. Mama spent a long time looking at the Hoosier kitchen cabinet, pointing out its good features to me as she discovered them. She pulled out the porcelain worktop, just the right size for rolling out a pie crust. She rolled back the doors in the middle to look at the revolving spice carousel, and at the sugar and floor bins with sifters on the bottom, where she could put down a measuring cup and sift right into it. She opened the doors above, where she could store our everyday dishes, and examined the narrow shelf on one door for vanilla and other flavorings.

I was busy looking in the drawer below the counter, where we could put sharp knives, stirring spoons, the potato masher, and the egg beater. Opening the doors below the drawer, I discovered shelves that pulled out for pots and pans and a rack on the door for pan lids. I could see that the top drawer on the right side was for silverware, but I had to ask Mama about the two drawers below, with metal linings and covers.

"Those are for cake and bread," she explained. "You pull the metal top over the food in the drawer, and that keeps it fresh."

"This is exactly what I'd like to have," Mama told Mr. Watterson, "but it's too expensive for us."

"That's the best one," Mr. Watterson agreed. "It's the Cadillac of cabinets."

We went back and looked at the other cabinets several times, but it was no use. Her heart's desire was the Hoosier.

Mama and Papa discussed the subject.

"It sounds mighty fine," Papa agreed. "I suppose it has a fine price on it, too."

"Well, it is the most expensive. I don't expect to get that one. An inexpensive one would do just as well. I don't need to have my every whim granted when other expenses have to be paid. I just want to keep the dishes closer to the place where they're used."

Papa listened to all this very soberly. "Yes, I can see that you're sensible and will be happy to have any cabinet at all. Why don't I nail up a few shelves above this old table you're using. That ought to work, and I can paint them like the woodwork."

Papa spoke so seriously, but I could see a twinkle in his eye.

"Oh, you!" Mama knew when she was being teased.

One late August day Papa took a load of oats to town to sell. As he left, he looked mighty pleased with himself and said to Mama, "I wonder what price these oats will bring today?"

She looked back at him as if that statement meant more than the words said. I was puzzled.

When Papa came home, we looked out the window and saw a big shape covered with a blanket in the grain wagon.

"Whatever that is, I'll be pleased with it," she whispered to me as he came in the door.

"I want you ladies to come out and see what found its way into my wagon," he said to us. We hurried out, and with undisguised delight, Papa swept off the blanket. There was the Hoosier!

"O-oh, Paul," Mama exclaimed, close to tears. "I didn't think you'd get that one."

"I got a good price for my oats." Papa spoke gruffly to hide his emotion.

A tender look passed between the two of them and was held for a long moment.

He went to get the hired man to help carry in the cabinet, and Mama hurried into the house to move the old table out of the way and clean the floor and wall where it had stood. Once the new cabinet was in place, she washed the shelves and drawers and put in the dishes she'd need right away.

"I almost forgot to get supper while I was putting things in the cabinet," she said as the men came in. "I could open a jar of fruit if this isn't enough."

"It's lucky there were a few leftovers for you to warm up for us hardworking men, eh, Harry?" Papa was still in a jovial mood after surprising Mama.

In the next few days Mama gradually emptied her spices into the jars on the carousel, filled the sugar and flour bins through the openings in the top shelf, and arranged and rearranged things in the cabinet until she was satisfied.

THE KITCHEN

Mama's first task each morning was to build a fire in the cookstove. She dumped in cobs, dashed on a small amount of kerosene, threw a lighted match on the cobs, and quickly stepped back before the flame leaped up. Satisfied that the cobs had caught fire, she put the round lid back on the stove top, then shoved sticks of wood through the front door.

When the men came in from early choring, she had perked coffee on the hot stove and pushed it back to keep warm. Pancakes or eggs, with bacon or sausages, sizzled in her heavy, black iron skillets. She drained extra grease into a ceramic jar between salt and pepper shakers in a little tray on the cool part of the stove. She toasted bread on the cook top, and we slathered it with butter and apple butter or jam. We had dinner, a meat and potatoes meal, at noon. Mama often boiled enough extra potatoes to slice and fry for supper in soft grease dipped from the handy container. Canned meat, vegetables, and fruit were added to both meals.

Sometimes in winter Mama filled her biggest kettle with soup bones and lots of water early in the morning. She brought it to a quick boil by lifting the round stove-top lid and setting the kettle directly over the flame. (Later she had to scrub soot off the bottom of the kettle.) Then she moved the kettle back on the stove to simmer all day. As the day wore on, Mama added vegetables: carrots, tomatoes, onions, potatoes, and often rice to thicken it. As the savory smell of the contents in the big kettle assailed our nostrils, she was apt as not to sing a chorus of "Who Put the Overalls in Mrs. Murphy's Chowder?"

Mama soured milk on the back of the barely warm stove and drained it through a sugar sack; with cream and salt added, it became cottage cheese. She baked pies: apple, elderberry, and green-tomato mince, and kept the cookie jar full. Homemade pudding or rice boiled with raisins and served with cream and sugar were simple desserts. Occasionally she set a sponge for bread in the evening, mixing lukewarm water, flour, yeast, and a little sugar. In the morning she added more flour to the bubbly mixture, kneaded it, and made it into loaves, then let it rise. When it was baked, she turned the fragrant loaves out of the pans, thumped them on the bottoms to listen for the hollow sound that meant they were done, and rubbed the crusts with a piece of bread wrapper dipped in butter. Nothing ever tasted better than the crusty heel of a loaf hot from the oven, spread thickly with butter Mama and I had churned in a barrel churn using our own sweet cream.

I baked my first cake when I was nine, a spice cake from Mama's *Inglenook Cook Book*. The recipe began, "Take lard the size of a duck egg, and two scant teacups of sugar." The cake was a success, and from then on I baked often: oatmeal and ginger cookies, and mahogany cake with powdered sugar frosting, often flavored with mint or black walnut.

The oven had a temperature gauge, but we didn't trust it. It was best to learn by experience to judge the oven's heat by the way it felt when you stuck your hand into it. Similarly, one had to learn how much fuel (cobs or wood) to put in the firebox to achieve the needed temperature for baking.

In the summer and fall we preserved many kinds of food: the canning, of course, and corn dried on the back of the stove in a big, flat pan, with the corn on top and hot water in an enclosed section of the pan underneath; when we butchered, sausage spiced just right for our taste and squeezed into casings that were the cleaned intestines of the butchered hog (I tried not to think of that when I ate the sausage), bacon and hams rubbed with salt and other preservatives and with liquid smoke for flavor.

A wainscot of vertically grooved boards topped with a ledge just the width of my foot covered the lower three feet of the kitchen wall. It was climbing height for me. If I put one foot on the ledge and "walked" my hands up the stairway door, just across the narrow hall, I could put one hand on the ceiling and grasp the woodwork of the pantry and front room doors. Mama never allowed anything to be set on this ledge, so I only had to watch out for the wall clock on its shelf between the two doors. It was warm up there, and it gave me a new perspective of the room. I considered myself very daring until I grew out of such jinks when I was about ten.

In this same area the boys wrestled on the floor, making a great pretense of hurting each other. As long as there was more laughter than cries of pain, Mama ignored their scuffling. When my younger brother, Dale, was about five, he and I enjoyed playing a game in which I'd push him down to the floor, hold his legs down with my knees, his hands with my hands, and swish my hair across his face, causing him to laugh helplessly.

Mama's dainty oak drop-leaf desk, built like a box on four slender legs, was in one corner of the kitchen. The slanted front of the desk opened down to make a writing table. On top of the desk was Grandpa Freem's picture. He was posed standing, looking dapper in a white outfit and a Panama hat. The gray velveteen bear that was lost when we moved should have been beside his picture.

Inside the desk was Mama's bamboo stamp box, which seldom contained stamps. It was one of my favorite playthings. She had bought it in Chinatown when she lived in California. It just fit into the palm of my hand as it widened and tapered to its top, following the shape of the bamboo stem from which it was made. It was not completely round at the top. The lid fit snugly into a ridge inside of the box, and it had to be put in exactly right, like a piece of a jigsaw puzzle. The lid lifted out with a mushroom-shaped handle. Sometimes I carelessly put it in upside down and then tried to pry it out with my fingernails. Small nicks around the lid attested to the times I had to release it with the point of a sharp knife.

I nestled the box in my hand, loving its satiny feel and golden color, trying to imagine the person who had fit the bottom in so carefully and carved the stylized figures into the lid. Were they birds, ships, a Chinese house, clouds? How did it happen that this box, carved in a land so far away, had been bought in California by my mother and had come to be in my hand in Iowa? Would Harry and I have found something like this exotic box if we had completed one of the holes we had started to dig through the earth to China?

The dining table was covered with brightly patterned oilcloth for everyday. When the oilcloth got too worn to look decent, Mama and I had the fun of choosing a new piece from the store. It brightened the room, and I liked the rubbery new smell. When we had guests, we put extra leaves in the table. Then Mama put one of her white, damask linen cloths on the table over a thick, fleecy white cloth called a silence cloth, the purpose of which was to silence the clatter of dishes and silver on the wooden table. The linen cloths and the big matching napkins were a nuisance to iron, but Mama took pride in using them.

Chairs were set all around the table, as many as needed for the people present. To save space, we children sat against the wall, with the table pushed as close to us as possible. Sometimes I was in the middle, with a brother on each side. To get out, I slithered to the floor, worked my way around table and human legs and made my escape.

At the slightest excuse we popped corn in a big kettle on a very hot stove, salted it generously, stirred lots of melted butter into it, and sat around the table eating and talking with our mouths full. My girl friends and I made fudge or crackling butterscotch candy and, while we waited for it to cool, played paper dolls, cutting dresses for them out of wall-paper sample books spread over the table. We played count-less games of Old Maid and Flinch, too, but were not allowed to use the sinful decks of regular playing cards.

Our family sat around the table in the evening with a kerosene lamp — later a much brighter Aladdin — in the mid-dle and read the paper, did our homework, wrote letters, and ate snacks of bread and cream and sorghum.

Behind the table was a window with sheer, white, dimity curtains. Mama kept her eyeglasses on the ledge in the middle of the window when she took them off for the night. After her death in 1936, I found them there. Seeing them brought a vivid, hurting picture to my mind, of her holding the glasses to her mouth to blow quick breaths on them ("huh-huh") and rubbing off the mist on a corner of her apron.

Our box telephone hung on the wall just south of the window. To use it, we took the receiver off the hook and listened to hear if anyone was using the party line. If the line was open, we rang Central (the operator) by turning the crank on the right side of the box. After she responded, "Number pull-eeze?" we gave the number and she rang the person. Families on party lines each had their own rings. For many years ours was long-short-long. We could ring people on our party line directly. Because we could hear all the rings on our line, we always knew who was being called. To listen in on other people's conversations, or "rubber," was consid-ered very poor manners, but the temptation was nearly im-possible to resist. Sometimes it served a purpose. If a family was known to have illness, we updated ourselves on the ill-ness without having to bother the family. Most people were realistic enough to know that others might hear any conversa-tion on a party line.

If a child played with the phone, or rubbered too long, many a parent chastised the child by saying, "If you don't quit rubbering, Central will cut off your ears."

When I was young, I thought she could do that right through the telephone line. Mama didn't threaten us with those words, so I didn't worry about losing my ears.

I did have one embarrassing contact with Central during the Depression of the thirties, when I was old enough to know better. So many people had their phones disconnected as an economy measure that Papa said, "There's hardly anyone left to call. We might as well take ours out, too."

We did that, though the telephone hung on the wall as usual, and we could hear the rings on the line. Once I wondered if our phone really was disconnected and I rang Central. She immediately responded, "Number, pull-eeze?"

In an embarrassed voice I said faintly "248," Aunt Jen's number. Her telephone also was disconnected.

"What number?" asked Central, but I wouldn't respond.

"Were you calling 'four-eight'? Does someone need the doctor. Are you hurt?"

"Four-eight" was Dr. Call's number, and the operator feared someone might be too ill to talk. She rang several people on the line before she gave up. Mama noticed that something was amiss, and I confessed. She scolded me sharply, saying the telephone was not a toy. I was sorry for my thoughtless curiosity.

Central knew more than anyone else about what was going on in the community and often imparted some of her knowledge to help callers. If someone called a doctor, she might say, "Dr. Call is at the Whites', and he probably won't be back in his office until the baby is born. Shall I ring another doctor for you?"

When an emergency occurred that everyone needed to know about, she rang a very long ring, called a "line ring," to alert people, one line after another. When this happened, we hurried to the phone, as our help might be needed with a fire or an accident.

During a phone call we had to stand and talk into a speaker attached to the phone box. We wrote messages on a slip of paper held against the slanted shelf on the front of the phone. I remember a cookie recipe Mama thus copied from Mrs. Johnson. They were called overnight cookies, and we could bake them only when the weather was cold enough to chill them outside overnight. It was a new idea.

Mama rocked her babies in a little armless chair, called a sewing rocker, in the space between the table and the stove. Once I asked for a child's rocker to rock my dolls. Mama said, "You can call this chair yours." I was satisfied with that promise, and the rocker was very special to me.

Ironing required the strength of an Amazon, but it seemed vitally important to do it well. Monday was wash day, and clothes to be ironed were starched, dried, sprinkled, rolled into tight cylinders, and stored in the wicker clothes basket. Mama ironed everything except rags and sheets. Tuesday morning, very early in hot weather, Mama shook out a piece to be ironed and smoothed it out on the ironing board. The heavy, solid irons, pointed at both ends (sometimes aptly called sadirons), were heating on the hot stove. Snapping the handle on an iron, she checked its temperature by touching the bottom with a just-licked finger. A quick sizzle meant it was hot enough. When this iron cooled as it was used, she returned it to the stove and picked up a hot one.

From the age of seven, I practiced ironing, starting with dish towels and handkerchiefs and progressing to the men's blue chambray work shirts, taking heed to Mama's instructions to press hard on the seams so they would be flat and smooth.

"Just look at the seams of a garment to see how well a woman irons," she advised me.

Ironing was accompanied by a smell of scorching, by steam billowing out of the garments under the iron, and by perspiration rolling down the ironer's face.

A teakettle always sang on the black and chrome kitchen range, offering instant hot water for a cup of tea or a hot water bottle. The well water we filled it with contained minerals, which precipitated out into the teakettle as the water steamed away. When it got heavy, we were reminded to scrape out some of the deposit—a good job for a young girl in the family. Once in awhile we had to buy a new teakettle and start over when it became impossible to get the lime out of the old one. The steam from the teakettle added needed moisture to the dry air in winter. On the right end of the stove a water reservoir (we pronounced it "rezavoy") heated soft cistern water, used for cleaning purposes, conveniently near our kitchen sink. We were sure few people had a handier arrangement.

At the kitchen sink we washed, brushed our teeth, shampooed our hair, combed it, did hand laundry, and Papa shaved here. We took our baths in a round laundry tub in front of the stove, with the oven door open for warmth in cold weather, glad to have the hot soft water to dip out of the reservoir. Lux soap was my favorite, and I felt dainty and fragrant after my weekly bath.

Wet mittens dried on the open oven door, warning us with a scorched wool smell if they got too hot. We propped our cold feet up there to warm and dry them. Sometimes Pa wrapped a runty pig in a towel and set it in a box near the heat. Mama discouraged that. She didn't like to have her kitchen smell like a hog house.

From this kitchen, where we lived so much of our lives, we went through its seven doors to our various activities.

THE UPSTAIRS HALL

Alone but not lonely, I spent many hours playing in our upstairs hall. As big as a room, it had an unfinished ceiling with beams like an attic. Rain pattered hypnotically on a metal part of this roof, washing out other sounds and creating in me a delightful feeling of isolation in the dry comfort of the hall. Sometimes it began in a hurry of little drips, plinking sounds like light fingers on a keyboard. Sometimes it went on to an urgent percussion of drops hitting a hard rat-a-tat-tat that ebbed and flowed with the wind. It was music to dream by.

This room had interesting storage places, inviting my imagination to whisk me away beyond my limiting world. A travel-worn steamer trunk with a broken strap and a clasp that didn't fasten set me to wondering on what trips it had accompanied my family. Mama had lived in California during her teen years. Did her treasures accompany her in this old trunk?

A helter-skelter box of pictures and two old picture albums were half hidden under the dusky eaves, but they didn't escape my searching eyes. Who were these people? How was I related to them?

A five-drawer chiffonier beckoned me to explore its contents. What was in each drawer, and why had Mama saved these particular things? The top drawer held Mama's company-best pillowcases, guest towels, and dresser scarves, embroidered with her small, even stitches, cutwork, and hemstitching. She had made these for her hope chest before she was married and took pride in using them for special occasions. When she tried to teach me to embroider so I could start a hope chest of my own, I rebelled. "Why do I have to embroider?" I complained. "My stitches don't look nice. I only like to do French knots."

"It takes practice," she encouraged me. "My stitches weren't so good, either, when I started to embroider. You'll like it better when you improve. You'll want to have things ready in your hope chest when you're married."

I glumly suspected that I might never get married if having a hope chest was one of the prerequisites.

Drawers were filled with baby clothes, all in white, in which I could dress my dolls. There were flannelette sacques and kimonos, with pastel ribbons to tie at the neck, dresses with their own gertrudes (slips), woolen navel bands, bonnets and booties, long stockings with pin holes worn in the tops, and tiny shirts with matching pin holes on the bottom, receiving blankets, and one fluffy crib-sized blanket with a satin binding. Many were the hours I dressed my dolls—Bobby, Dorothy, and Richard—in these interesting garments, and

dressed them again, planning trips we would take w
were finally ready.

In the bottom drawer were three long, exquisitely
child's dresses. They were long enough for me but too tight,
when I discovered them at about the age of five or six. I
puzzled over these and put them back until one day I found,
in the picture box, pictures of several babies wearing long
dresses like these. Who were they, and were these the dresses
in the drawer? Pictures in hand, I went down to ask Mama to
solve this puzzle for me.

She was rocking my little brother, Dale, in the low, armless rocker in the kitchen, softly singing a hymn, "There is a
Balm in Gilead." I told her I thought these little babies must
have been uncomfortable, wearing such long dresses. With a
smile, she explained that they were called christening dresses,
and babies wore them only when they were baptized or had
their pictures taken. Both boys and girls wore them for those
occasions. Taking two of the pictures in hand, she said that
one was her baby picture and the other was mine. I looked at
them a long time. We were wearing the same dress!

"Why didn't I have a new dress?" I demanded to know.

"I wanted to dress you as my mother had dressed me,"
she answered. "Besides, I couldn't have made you a dress
more beautiful than that one."

For the first time I thought about the generations that
went on, one after another. I hoped that someday I would
have a baby girl who could wear that same dress and have her
picture taken.

I gradually came to know the faces and most of the
names of the people in the pictures. One day I took a picture
of a group of people to Mama and asked her who these people were, standing in front of the church. Mama, who was
peeling potatoes, dried a hand and took the picture from me,
looking lovingly at it. She didn't answer me.

"Who are they, Mama? Tell me who they are. Why did
they have their pictures taken in front of the church? And
what does that sign in the front mean?"

"We were a Sunday School class, and we wanted to remember the Christian love we felt for one another. The sign says 'PLUS ULTRA.' It means 'the best,' and that's what we thought we were. Do you see anyone you know in the picture?"

"Can I have a bite of potato?"

"You may have a bite."

"I see you. Is Papa in the picture?"

"Of course he is. Don't you know your own father?" she teased me. "And here's Percy Lucas, and his sisters Gertrude and Genie. We were friends when we were little, no bigger than you. Our parents were good friends, too. As you know, we're still friends."

"Did you know Pa when you were a little girl?"

"No, he didn't live in Greene then. I met him in this very Sunday School class. He had come from Pennsylvania not long before. Believe me, when I met Paul Ott, I was glad we'd moved back to Greene!"

Another day, looking in the trunk, I found a strange-looking flat beaded purse, a spiky white pen holder, and some old-fashioned white pointed shoes. The very best treasure of all was under the sagging tray of the trunk. It was a pure white dress made of a soft material, in a lady's size. It had small tucks on the bodice and skirt, and lace and embroidery on the bodice. The skirt was softly gathered onto the waist. I had to ask Mama about this dress and see if I could play dress-up with it.

"Tell me about this dress, Mama."

"That's my wedding dress."

"Why did you wear such an old-fashioned dress?" I asked, wanting to think she had looked her best.

"It was right in style when we were married in 1914. Styles change all the time."

"Why did you save the dress? Are you going to wear it again sometime?"

"I didn't save it to wear. It makes me happy to see it and remember our wedding day." She paused, and then murmured, "I want to be buried in my wedding dress."

I turned my mind away from that statement. Mama must never leave me.

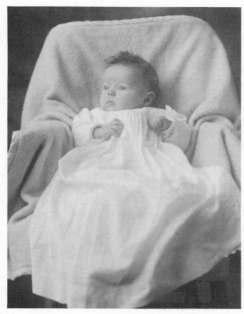

Margaret Ott,
age three months.

Sunday School Class. Top row: Dorotha Beal (second from left), Genie Lucas (sixth from left). Second row from top: Harry Downs (tall man below center window), Paul Ott (right, looking over Harry's shoulder), Percy Lucas (right; third row man appears to be between Paul and Percy). Harry Downs and Genie Lucas later married and their daughter Lucille was Margaret's friend.

"Where's your wedding picture? Is it in the box?"

"I have a picture in my mind's eye, and that's enough for me. We talked it over and decided to use the money that pictures would have cost to help furnish our home." She was quiet for a long time, and seemed to forget me. Then she said, "Paul and I have a dream. We want to have our own farm someday. We can go without things now, to save for that." Mama didn't live to see it, but the dream came true for Papa.

"And, no, you may not play dress-up with my wedding dress."

"I'll put it back in the trunk upstairs very carefully right now," I promised.

THE BACK KITCHEN

The back kitchen was a passageway between the kitchen and the outside door. In the hottest weather we cooked simple meals on a three-burner kerosene stove in this room. A typical meal consisted of canned beef, fresh fried potatoes, boiled green beans and sliced tomatoes from our garden, and perhaps a cake baked in the square, black tin oven that sat on one burner (its temperature regulated by experience), covered with a simple frosting made by boiling brown sugar and thick cream together. We ate on a scarred old table with one short leg and a leaf warped out of shape, moved in front of the north window.

Because it was dressed up in a simple cloth, with a glass I had stuffed with zinnias sitting in the center, I thought this table took on airs as if it were the fine lady in the house and the oilcloth-covered dining table in the kitchen were the poor relation. It seemed festive to me, like a picnic, to eat in the back kitchen with odd chairs and a stool to sit on, relaxed and temporary.

On the west wall was a sink large enough for bathing a child, with a drain that no longer worked, and a pump to draw water from the cistern. Mama jokingly said you had to hold your mouth right to make the aged pump work. I liked the challenge and could almost always conquer it. First, I poured water brought from the kitchen down the pump to prime it, which soaked and swelled the dried leather gasket and created a vacuum. Then, as I pumped vigorously, the brackish water gushed into my pail. I rushed to empty this water into the reservoir on the end of the kitchen stove and hurried back so the water would continue to flow as I pumped.

This yellowish, swampy-smelling water was not for drinking, as it was collected in the cistern from rain that ran off the roof into the eaves troughs. We liked this water for all kinds of cleaning because it was soft and soap did not leave a scum in it. Mama didn't use the cupboard under the sink, with its doors that had to be pried open, but gave it up to the mice and the cobwebs.

Next to the sink was a door that opened into the wood-shed. Through this door our Maytag washing machine was pulled into the back kitchen in the winter. When I complained of the smell of the gasoline-powered motor, Mama said to me, "Count your blessings, Margaret. If it weren't for that smelly motor, we'd be moving the agitator and turning the wringer by hand. I can tell you that is very hard work." I was always glad when it warmed up and we could wash in the better ventilated woodshed again.

Monday was wash day, and I often helped by chipping the hard homemade soap onto a paper and dumping it into the water heating in the copper boiler on the stove, then dipping the hot mixture into the square gray tub of the washer. I liked to run the clothes through the wringer, after Mama decreed they had agitated long enough. I lifted the steaming clothes with a laundry stick — a bleached and worn length cut from the handle of an old broom — to the revolving hard rubber cylinders of the wringer.

Mama warned me about using my fingers to stick an edge of the clothes into the wringer, telling me horror stories of women who had caught their fingers or hair in it and been drawn into the wringer before they could get it stopped. That little thrill of danger kept me alert.

The wringer pivoted on a post on the machine so we could wring the clothes through the two rinses into round galvanized tubs filled with cold water and set on backless chairs, and finally into the oval brown wicker clothes basket. Mama put bluing into the second rinse to whiten the laundry. White clothes were washed first, then successively darker loads were washed and rinsed in the same waters. Mama instructed me that it should be a housewife's pride to have the whitest wash, hung out the earliest of anyone in the neighborhood. After the washing was done, she used the wash water and an old broom to scrub the woodshed, the back porch, and the outside toilet.

In the spring newly hatched chicks shrilly peep-peeped in cardboard boxes set on the table and in the sink, waiting to be moved to the brooder house north of the grove. During the three weeks of their incubation, I had sometimes helped Mama turn the eggs daily in the incubator sitting in the warmest upstairs bedroom, where the pipe of the heating stove went through on its way to the roof. I had seen the eggs as they were pipped, and seen the chicks emerge, wet and naked-looking. By the time we moved them to the back kitchen, they were fluffy little yellow balls, still rounded from the nourishing egg that had produced each, so soft to cuddle in my hands.

I would have been happy to keep them in the back kitchen longer, but after the second day, when all the eggs were hatched, Mama said the papers in their boxes were getting wet and smelly and, besides, she was tired of their incessant peeping. They belonged in the brooder house north of the grove, where they could move around as they grew. This brooder house had a low hood that hovered over the baby chicks like the wings of many hens.

After fall butchering Mama made soap with fat rendered out of butchering scraps, as well as that saved all year from cooking. The process started in the back yard by the granary, where Mama hung the big black kettle on a tripod over a fire. The fat was scraped into the kettle from the various storage containers where it had been accumulating, and cans of Lewis Lye and water were added. Mama stirred it with a long, narrow, wooden board that Papa had shaped for this purpose. After a long time she ladled it into cardboard boxes lined with newspapers.

"How do you know when it's done, Mama?" I asked.

"I've cooked it so many times that I can tell by the way it stirs. Usually I'm about right, but it took lots of practice to learn when it was done."

The boxes were set in the sink and on the table in the back kitchen. As soon as it began to set up, but before it was hard, she cut it into oblong chunks, using her heaviest butcher knife. When it was dry and shrunken into strange shapes, she turned it out onto more papers and peeled off the newspaper from the bottom. We could never get it all off, and the soap always had shreds of paper clinging to it. I picked at it until the strong soap got under my fingernails and hurt and the caustic fumes made me sneeze.

In the winter a clutter of outer wear hung on hooks in one corner of the back kitchen. On the floor were galoshes, Papa's black rubber knee boots smelling of barnyard dirt, a broom to brush off snow before we came in, a redolent kerosene lantern. Mama put down newspapers after she had mopped the area with wash water every Monday, but there was no way to control the mess. Its familiarity made it invisible to us.

THE PANTRY

Before doors were built to hide the pantry shelves, I was curious to see what I could only glimpse from the floor. I inched a chair from the kitchen to the pantry and crawled up to snoop. Most interesting was a drinking glass with a heavy frosted coating. In it was a necklace of gold beads with a broken string. I asked Mama if she was going to fix it.

"M-m-m," she answered absently as she hung a freshly washed curtain over the pantry window. "Maybe, someday when I have time."

When I looked for it later, the glass and the necklace were gone. I never asked Mama about it, afraid she would tell me she had thrown it out on the junk heap behind the hen house. I preferred to believe, as I did with my bear, that it would come to light some day. Maybe it was in the safe deposit box in the bank. Gold beads were surely valuable.

Mama enlisted my help in getting supper ready to celebrate Grandpa's eighty-third birthday, when I was seven. She lifted her long, white, damask linen tablecloth from its drawer in the pantry, we each took an end of it, and, holding it taut, we settled it down over the silence cloth already smoothed out on the table.

She handed me the celery dish, a long, narrow bowl with Oriental designs painted on it, to carry to the table, and she carried her cut glass cream and sugar set. As she did, she told me that this was one of her most cherished possessions. Her Great Uncle Frank and Aunt Lillian had given it to Papa and Mama as a wedding gift. What made it so special was that Aunt Lillian had carried it on her lap on the train all the way from Maine so it wouldn't get broken.

"Now choose a plate to put the bread on. We'll do it up fancy tonight," she directed me.

"Where did you get these plates, Mama?" I asked. I was interested after hearing the story about the cut glass set.

"They were wedding presents, too, given to us by friends who had painted them. China painting was a popular hobby for ladies in 1914."

I took my favorite plate off the shelf, one with pale pink leaves, shadowy mauve flowers, and a gold filigree border. Watching how careful Mama was when she washed these dishes, I was equally careful when I dried them.

Earlier that day she had baked a white layer cake and had sent me to the pantry to get the tall, crystal cake stand to set it on. That made it seem even more like a party, because we usually had our angel food birthday cakes on this plate.

Mama gave me the lowest wide drawer, under the tablecloths, to use for my own. I kept scrapbooks there, the ones Mama made for me from store wrapping paper. She cut several pages the same size, pressed them flat, and stitched them down the middle on her sewing machine. When she folded the pages on the stitching, there was my new tablet or scrapbook. I had filled a couple of these with pictures cut from magazines, pasted down with flour and water paste. When I saw the black calling cards left by the mice, and the nibbles on my *Johnny Jingles* book, I knew why Mama had so generously given me this drawer. Still, I liked having a private place, and mice were too familiar to worry about.

Harry and I each had a narrow drawer. His was filled with junk: stones he liked, marbles, a top, and stuff he emptied out of his pockets.

Mine held valuables: the magnet Mama gave me when I was in the hospital in Des Moines after getting sick at the State Fair, Crackerjack prizes—a little purple glass kitten, a metal puzzle with sharp edges that sliced my finger if I wasn't careful. A glance at a pink pot holder reproached me for my second-grade ineptitude in sewing. I was supposed to make the pot holder as a gift for Mama, but I continually made excuses for not working on it. I hated doing it because my stitches looked so awful. The teacher finally gave up and finished it herself, but I never gave it to Mama. I kept it because it would be wasteful to throw away something new.

In this drawer, too, were the little bird cards Mama gave me from boxes of Arm and Hammer soda. They had descriptions of the birds on the back, and they came in cellophane envelopes. I was careful to keep every one, and I had them framed more than fifty years later for a son-in-law who likes to watch birds.

The best of my treasures was a pair of silver scissors, not more than 1-1/2 inches long, with blades that really worked. Papa brought it for me from Chicago, where he had gone with a load of cattle to sell in the big stockyards.

When Pa had stock to sell, he watched the daily paper to see what prices the buyers were paying. He could look at a feedlot of cattle or hogs, apply some seemingly magic formula in his head, and estimate their weight within a few pounds. When they reached the best weight and the price was right, he would book passage for them on the evening freight train to Chicago, and for himself in the train's caboose. He would gather up a crew to drive the livestock to town: my brothers, the hired man, and a few neighbors. Sometimes I was called upon to help guard the driveways of farm homes we passed on our way to town, shouting and waving my arms to keep the animals on the road.

The animals were kept in the pens by the tracks until the train picked them up for the overnight ride. We took Papa, with his satchel and a lunch Mama had packed for him, to town to catch the same train. The caboose was a small red car at the very end of the train. It was used by the train crew as an office, and for passengers like Papa who had a reason to be on the train. On the top of the car was a cupola, so the trainman could look out over the freight cars ahead in the train. A pipe sticking out of the roof was attached to a stove in the caboose. It looked very interesting, but I never had a chance to board the car to look it over. Papa said it wasn't comfortable to ride but it took him where he needed to go.

When they arrived at the stockyards, Papa met with the

buyers and made the best deal he could. He came home with tales to tell of the noisy, smelly stockyards, and the rough men to whom he turned over his stock. It sounded like a frightening adventure. He usually brought us each a small gift, a treat we didn't expect every day.

In another of the narrow drawers Mama kept her flour sack dish towels, the company best ones carefully folded at the bottom and everyday ones on top. She washed her dish towels in the first load of washing, in the cleanest and hottest water. She taught me that a good housekeeper must always keep her dish towels white and spotless.

When a forty-nine-pound white cotton flour sack was empty, I'd take it outside, turn it wrong side out and shake it and shake it to get out all the flour. Then I picked at the stitches until I found the one thread to pull that would un-ravel all the stitching on the side and bottom of the sack. Mama rubbed the printing with her strong lye soap, soaked the sack in boiling water, and left it on the clothesline in the hot summer sun to bleach. Our dish towels never had traces of print on them to betray their humble origin. Mama hemmed them and sometimes embroidered a little design in one corner.

Dish towels had a third stage of use. When they were ragged, but soft and lintless, they were valuable to polish lamp chimneys, mirrors, and windows. They were just right to tear into strips for bandaging a stubbed toe or a cut. We kept these in the rag drawer. Just so it would be handy, we kept in this drawer a ball of string, to which we continually added more from store packages.

When I saw Mama's deep, round, layer cake pans on a shelf, my tongue hurt. I remembered the day Papa's brothers, Uncle Frank and Uncle Ross, brought them. They came to visit us in 1920, after they got out of army. The pans were very special because they'd had them made by a tinsmith in their hometown in Pennsylvania, just for Mama. "The boys," as my parents called my uncles, had lived with us before the war, while they decided whether they should move to Iowa, and Mama had been good to them. I remember the day they brought the pans because I had been in such a fever of excitement at the thought of visitors that I jumped up and down on the couch and bit my tongue.

On a high shelf on the south wall sat a row of staples: a sack of salt, "Chocolate Cream" coffee in a round, waxy, cardboard box, Post Toasties with a picture of a fireplace and a cat on the front of the box, Grapenuts (the only other cold cereal Mama ever bought), oatmeal, and dried fruits. I liked to reach into the sack and slip out a few tasty dried apricots, their edges curling like little ears. I had to know when to stop, because Mama wasn't happy to find an empty sack on the shelf. I liked raisins, too, but didn't trust them after I found little white worms crawling in them one hot summer day. On the same shelf Pa kept a spare box of Prince Albert pipe tobacco, a thin, red box with rounded corners just right to slide easily into a back overall pocket.

Under this shelf were hooks to hang our good coats, sweaters, and caps. Mama kept a clean apron on the hook nearest the door, to exchange hurriedly for a dirty one if we saw unexpected company coming in the driveway. Aprons were indispensable to Mama and her friends — to use as a pot holder, or to help open a jar.

Behind the door were Papa's rifles and shotgun. They were seldom used. In the winter he sometimes shot a couple of nice rabbits, or a pheasant or two. The fresh game was a welcome change from our canned beef and pork, but I hated to bite down on a shotgun pellet when Mama had missed one as she cleaned the meat.

Whenever a loud squawking from the hen house announced that a four-footed marauder was intent on a midnight meal of chicken, Pa took out his rifle and shot into the air to frighten away the thief, usually a 'coon. I often roused at the commotion but went right back to sleep. Though the guns were seldom used, I got a fine feeling of security to know they were there.

In warm weather we pulled the washtub into the pantry to take a bath with the door closed for more privacy than usual. This allowed for more leisurely baths.

On the west wall was a drop-down table, higher than a regular table, which folded flat against the wall when not in use. A hinged leg at the bottom fit into a wooden slot on the wall and held the table in place when it was being used. Mama often cooled a pie or a few loaves of bread there, or hung a bag of acidy smelling cottage cheese to drain, out of the way.

In November of 1937, I stood here with my cousin Eunice, leaning against the table, looking out the window and listening to the auctioneer sell our possessions. Pa had decided to move back to Pennsylvania after Mama died. It is the last memory I have of being in this house.

THE FRONT ROOM

In summer the living room was seldom used except by me. Often I curled up on the brown mohair sofa or its matching chair, if the summer day wasn't so hot that the mohair scratched my bare skin. The books I borrowed weekly at the library (only four at a time were allowed) were soon devoured. Over and over I read Mama's copy of *The Five Little Peppers and How They Grew*; *Jed, the Poorhouse Boy* and other Alger books borrowed from our neighbors; and a humorous book of Mama's, *Officer 666*. The first line of this book read, "Splash! the grapefruit hit her in the eye."

The door of the living room was often kept closed and the roller shades pulled down over the three closed windows, in hopes of keeping out dust from the dirt road and keeping the room cool. The men worked long days in the fields, and if we sat down to relax awhile before bedtime, it was usually outdoors or on the front porch.

During spring housecleaning Mama rolled up the floral Axminister rug, leaving the linoleum beneath it bare for the summer. She had Papa or the hired man carry the rug out to the clothesline, where she attacked the dirt with her wire carpet beater. The winter's accumulation of dust billowed out in clouds as she began to beat it. When Harry and I got old enough, we took our turns whacking away. Then the rug was turned to the other side and the beating continued. During the winter Mama frequently ran her Bissell carpet sweeper over the rug, and sometimes she swept it with a broom dipped lightly in water, but the only way to get out the ground-in dirt was to beat it out. When we could see no more dust coming out, the rug was taken down, rolled up firmly, covered with papers, and stored in the woodshed until fall.

One spring when the wool rug was taken up, the linoleum was cracked and curling up around the edges, so Mama bought a new linoleum rug. Between the rug and the wall was a strip of wood-grained floor covering about thirty inches wide, pretending to be an oak floor. After the rug was rolled out and furniture spaced to help make it lay flat, Mama asked me to discard the wrappings. Among them I noticed two little five-inch diameter, round wooden posts, about five inches high. They had been inserted into the ends of the roll to protect the rug. I thought there must be some way I could play with them and decided to try to walk on them. I cut strips of rubber from an old inner tube and used these across my feet and under the posts to hold them on. After some practice I could stump all around the yard on these little stilts. They weren't as good as the roller skates I longed for but couldn't use because we had no cement in our yard, but these discards gave me a lot of pleasure. I felt rather smug that I had figured out how to make these "walkers" all by myself.

Spring was wallpapering time, and Mama had some of the rooms papered every couple of years. For a long time the front room was papered with a tiresome "oatmeal paper." The name well described the color, texture, and design.

Mama liked it because, as she said, "It's a good background for pictures."

She especially meant two enlarged and framed snapshots of Robert, taken in our front yard, attired only in a diaper. In one he was sitting up, looking sober, and in the other he was lying on his stomach on a blanket, laughing. Mama had taken them when he was a year old, a month before he died. She said again and again how thankful she was to have those pictures.

When the oatmeal paper began to look dingy around the doors and behind the stove and loosened where the pieces joined, Mama decided it must be repapered. After that decision was made, we children were allowed to tear at the tempting loose pieces, which had to come off anyway before new paper was put on. I conjectured about the layers thus exposed, and my relatives who had lived there so many years. Had Aunt Jen chosen the brown lattice paper with the green leaves? Had this pretty pattern with soft pink roses been on the wall when Thomas came to court Bertha, the youngest daughter in the family? Would someone in the years ahead know I lived here when the oatmeal paper was on the wall? I hoped no one would think I had liked it!

Mama brought wallpaper sample books from the store, and we chose a stylized design of feathery soft green ferns. The paperhanger came with his ladders and bench and brushes. First he cooked the paste. After Mama convinced him that she was capable of cooking the starch-water mixture to his exacting requirements, she did this the next day before he got there, so it was cooled and he could start pasting right away. He measured out the paper, allowing for that mysterious measurement he called "the match." Mama and the store clerk had discussed this, so she had bought enough paper for it. He spread the paper out on his bench and brushed the paste over all of it. He folded it paste side in, carried it as he climbed up his ladder, and lifted it to the top of the wall. The first strip had to go in a line with a piece of string he hung down from the ceiling — his plumb line, he called it. He chuk-

chukked the paper with a wide brush close to the ceiling. Then, slick as could be, he unfolded the rest of the paper in sections until he had the whole strip in place. He looked it over carefully to be sure it was perfectly in line with his string.

Succeeding strips went on with the same care. I looked on quietly, and he didn't seem to mind a watcher who admired him as if he were a magician. If there was a small bubble, he took care to work it out before he went on. I liked the quick way he brushed up and down the strips, making sure that each firmly adhered to the wall. After the ceiling and walls were done, he put a border close to the ceiling on the walls, giving them a finished look. I had heard people use the expression "Busier than a one-handed paperhanger with the itch." Watching this man at work, I could see that that would be busy indeed.

He and Mama sometimes visited as he worked, and she seemed to enjoy it. But, when he took a meal with us and fastidiously cut out the few tiny black "eyes" that Mama had missed when she peeled the potatoes, she was upset. While we did dishes after he had gone, she sputtered to me, "He didn't need to take out those little specks. They wouldn't hurt anyone." She was silent for a moment and then said, "Well, I know he's persnickety, but that's a good trait in a paperhanger." She said she did like the neat way he papered, with the patterns perfectly matched and the paper tight and smooth on the wall; that was the important thing. The wet paste and paper smell and the soft feeling of the humidity it put into the room were pleasant. The fresh new paper let in spring.

When I was twelve, I remember lying on the cool-feeling linoleum on summer afternoons with my baby brother, Dean, singing him to sleep. Mama once had told me, when I was caterwauling away as I played the piano, that I should cease my noise and that I couldn't carry a tune anyway. I was very sensitive about it, but I thought if I made up a song, I could carry the tune anywhere I chose. One such forgettable song went:

Byelow, byelow, baby, go to sleep, I say.
Byelow, byelow, baby, go to sleep today.

How this affected Mama she never said, but the door between us was shut, and, besides, I was helping her with the baby. I did not think that Dean meant it as a critical comment when my singing put him to sleep.

When we got a radio in 1928, our horizons were broadened. It was an Atwater Kent cabinet model, and it filled the southeast corner of the front room. A battery as big as the one in our car furnished the power for it. The trouble was that the battery ran down frequently, usually when it was time for a favorite program to come on. It had to be taken into town and recharged, and that was not always convenient. Still, we heard most of the good programs, and that meant I could talk with the girls at school about Amos 'n Andy, and Fibber McGee and Molly. When I remember those programs now, I see them as if they had been on television.

After we got the radio, we left the door open on cool mornings because we liked to hear the "Music Shop" from WOI, Ames. This program was the chief influence on my musical education during my childhood years. I liked learning about music when the announcer made comments about the next piece to be played. There was a very old and faint record of the great tenor, Caruso, one of the famous Madame Schumann-Heink, and one of Galla Curci, a soprano. The commentator wondered if her singing was sharp or the flute accompanying her was flat. He thought such a famous singer could hardly be sharp.

Afternoons, we often listened to WNAX, Yankton, South Dakota, to the music of a little known band led by Lawrence Welk. Sometimes he was joined by Myron Floren, another accordionist. They played cheerful music, but I got very tired of "Clarinet Polka."

When the weather turned cool, the rug and the heating stove were brought in from the woodshed. After the rug was smoothed down, the stove was placed on a fireproof mat along the west wall of the front room. It was set up so the stovepipe went through a metal-lined hole in the ceiling to the bedroom above, and from there through the roof. We fed this stove from a coal pail that sat beside the stove, filled with wood that Papa had cut, sawed, and split into chunks to fit into the stove. To keep this stove performing at its best took skill. If too much wood was put in, or if the damper on the stovepipe was left open too long, the stove could get dangerously red hot. If not enough wood was put in at night when Pa banked the fire, it went out completely before morning. He occasionally used coal at night in the coldest weather, to keep the fire alive longer. I enjoyed playing behind the stove, the warmest spot in the room.

Taking out the ashes was a messy job. First the ashes had to be shaken down, using a poker in the grate, a dust-making procedure. Then the ashes were scraped into a pail, often with a hot coal or two still in them. It was no job for a novice.

The December I was eight, I was home for several days, fretful and bored, with an earache and a bad cold. Mama was sympathetic and said, "I'm going to give you something to play with, but you and I will have to keep it a secret."

Intrigued, I agreed to that condition. She brought out a big box and expectantly watched me open it. In it was a beautiful doll, dressed in a pink dress, bonnet, and bloomers, all trimmed with lace. Of course I was thrilled.

"You can play with her in the daytime, but when it is time for Harry to come home from school, we will have to put her away. Santa is going to bring her to you for Christmas." It was fun to have the doll, whom I named Dorothy, to play with, but most of all I remember the conspiracy between Mama and me, and her understanding of my need for something to do. On Christmas morning I was not disappointed to receive a gift I'd already played with.

I had frequent earaches, but there was little anyone could do to relieve them. Papa held me on his lap and while he smoked his pipe, blew warm smoke in my ear. This didn't really help the pain, but I liked the feeling it gave me to be snuggled in his lap. He didn't often hold me. Sometimes Mama dropped warm oil into my aching ear, but that didn't help either. One time I became deaf for several days from a bad ear infection. It was scary not to know when someone came into the small bedroom off the front room until my eyes told me.

One day when I was getting better, Mama rolled the piano out from the wall to clean behind it. I walked behind it and saw in that space a delightful playhouse. Mama agreed to leave the piano that way for awhile. It was an appreciated respite from the misery I had been enduring. There were little shelves on the back, in the construction of the piano. I must have had doll dishes to use, and Mama may have supplied me with small items to play with. During this time my ear "broke" and drained, and I gradually got my hearing back. I spent more time in bed with cotton in my ears, but the worst was past. Mama put the piano back where it belonged. Several other times I asked her to pull out the piano, but she never would.

Mama told me that when she was a little girl, she had enjoyed taking piano lessons, and I understood that she was a good piano student. When she was eight or nine, it was discovered that she was very much in need of glasses. When she got them, she was surprised to see that the piano notes were black. The notes had always looked red to her before.

The finish on our piano was sort of rough all over. Mama said that the varnish had "crazed" because the piano had been shipped across the desert twice, first when they moved to California and then when they moved back to Iowa. Our piano had a distinctive mellow sound that I liked and never found in another one.

For several summers I took piano lessons. I didn't progress as fast as my friends who took lessons year around and thought it was my lack of musical ability. As a grown-up I understood why I didn't learn as much in three months as others did in eleven or twelve months.

Like most children, I didn't like to practice. Mama used to sit on the piano bench and insist that I do so. She didn't like to make me do something I didn't want to do, but she persisted, saying again and again, "Someday you'll thank me for this." She was right.

Once in awhile Mama sat down to play in the evening. Sometimes Papa came and sat by her and they sang as she played:

We were sailing along,
On Moonlight Bay. . . .

It was a song that had been popular in their courting days. She often played "Red Wing" (my pretty little Red Wing), about an Indian girl, and songs ("K-K-K-Katie," and "Over There") from the World War that ended when I was a baby. Once in awhile she bought a new piece of sheet music, and I could play well enough to pick out the tune and sing it.

Mr. Phillips, the itinerant piano tuner, called us when he came to Greene. He and Mama discussed the advisability of having our piano tuned while he was in town and came to a mutual agreement. When he did come, he took off the front of the piano and exposed the strings. He was just tall enough to be able to strike the keys and reach the strings in the back of the piano. He played one note again and again and adjusted the strings according to some sound he was hearing that I certainly couldn't hear. Every note came in for the same treatment. Finally he would ripple off a lot of notes, play some chords, and listen some more. No wonder one of his shoulders was higher than the other and he walked with a limp, having to stand hour after hour, day after day, working in this position.

When he was satisfied with his work, and Mama agreed that she was satisfied, he glued on the ivory keys we had dislodged since his last trip and replaced any that were missing with new, whiter ones. If it was close to mealtime, Mama asked him to stay. He politely refused but did accept a cup of tea with sugar, and Mama always had it ready for him and poured herself a cup. They visited as they drank their tea, Mama paid him, and he went on his way. He appeared like some genie out of a bottle, and disappeared, and I wondered if he had a home and family or if he just went around and around, wraithlike, tuning pianos.

THE FRONT PORCH

Mornings, after my chores were done, I often lay on the couch in the screened-in front porch and listened to the mourning doves coo their melancholy syllables from the box elder tree, heard the leaves of the many trees whispering in the breeze, saw the sun shining through, making odd-shaped little shadows on the porch. In these quiet moments of my growing-up years, I felt a longing, a need for something to touch my emotions, to catch hold of my mind and challenge it, a need to be doing something worthwhile. During these times I would daydream about the future shape of my life. Often enough I was brought back to reality.

"Margaret, go get some rhubarb [we called it pie plant]," Mama would call out.

I took a pan and knife from the kitchen and went out to the garden. The sun warmed my back, and the crisp rhubarb crackled as I pulled it from its plant and cut off its big leaves. A juicy taste of the acid rhubarb bit my mouth and made my jaws ache. Curious cattle in the adjoining barnyard lopped their heads over the fence, releasing the rank smell of crushed weeds growing on the fence. Their frisky calves bobbed awkwardly up and down on their stiff legs as I stood watching them. Bees buzzed among the plants and sipped nectar for the hive. Golden butterflies floated on weightless wings around me.

The daydreams dissipated, and I was content with life at this moment. As I left the rhubarb in the kitchen, Mama teased, "It took you long enough. Did you go to China to get that rhubarb?"

"No," I answered, "but it pulled so hard I thought a

Chinaman might have 'hold of the roots." I grabbed two cookies and a book and went out to the porch again.

I couldn't have been more than five when our family sat on the porch one late afternoon during a storm, and thunder followed lightning so quickly that we knew it struck close. When Pa saw men running in the field south of us and realized a man on a plow had been hit, he hurried to the car to go help. I began to cry loudly as he was leaving, and he ran back to see if I was hurt. When he learned I was having a tantrum because I wanted to go with him, he gave me a talking-to I never forgot. Glaring at me, he said "Stop that screaming right now! Never cry that way when there's nothing wrong." His voice and mien were so fierce that I thought he might strike me. I never cried again to get my own way. Mama held me on her lap and soothed and calmed me as the rockers creaked on the wooden floor. She explained that my cries had frightened Papa, and that was why he was so severe with me. When he came home, Papa told us that the man on the plow had been killed instantly by the lightning.

When Pa had livestock or grain to sell, he sat on the front porch to read the market news in the paper, which came in the mail. To see Papa, who seemed to work all the time, sit in apparent idleness in the middle of the morning seemed strange.

On many summer days Mama and I sat companionably on the porch shelling peas or cutting green beans, away from the hot stove in the kitchen, where the copper boiler was being heated to process the jars when they were filled. And Mama bought lugs and baskets of fruit in season: peaches, cherries, lovely yellow Bartlett pears, and apricots. As we prepared them for canning, I liked to pop an inviting morsel into my mouth. Mama always chided me, "These aren't to eat now. Think how good they'll taste in the winter. We'll buy more to eat, but when we're in the canning business, we must can them all." She never did buy enough to satisfy me.

She cooked the fruits in hot sugar syrup and slipped them in an attractive pattern into jars that had been sterilized by boiling them upside down in a pan of water on the stove.

She poured hot syrup through the canning funnel to fill the jars, and wiped excess syrup off the tops. Then she put on the red rubber jar rings, tightened the zinc lids over them, and set them upside down to cool. Fruits did not have to be processed in the boiler. She let the jars sit overnight to be sure they were sealed. After each batch Mama sat on the porch with me, fanning herself and wiping away sweat. When they were cool and standing upright, the filled jars gleamed temptingly, promising sweet treats in the winter when fruit was out of season. I saw in Mama's face the satisfaction she felt at her accomplishment.

After supper we sat and chatted while it grew dark and the lightning bugs zig-zagged outside. The boys liked to catch them and put them in empty peanut butter jars. Sometimes friends stopped by, and I lay on the couch going in and out of sleep as I listened to the voices of the grown-ups murmuring. At times they sat in peaceful silence, just enjoying the rest.

THE BEDROOM

Our parents' bedroom, south of the kitchen, was their private domain; we children did not enter it without a reason. It was, therefore, a treat to rest in the oak wooden bed, with its old-fashioned tall headboard, when I was sick. On one such occasion I spent a few days there easing a sore throat by sucking on hard, round cherry drops (and developing cavities). Papa even bought me a second sack of them when he had an errand in town, making me feel uncommonly pampered.

This was the most cheerful room in the house, with windows on three sides, giving me a view of the road, the driveway, and the west yard.

Anna and John Ott, Paul Ott's parents.

Just to be in the room was a comfort, so close to Mama working in the kitchen, and near her most personal things. On the dresser lay her silver-backed dresser set: a comb, brush, and mirror, the heavily embossed backs in need of polishing. Mama was faithful in following the good grooming rule of that time, brushing her hair one hundred strokes every evening. When the brush wore out and she bought a new one from the Fuller Brush man, the silver one still lay on the dresser. I thought it added a touch of luxury to the room.

Mama's gallstones, removed in an operation in Rochester, Minnesota, when I was eight, were in an oblong cardboard box in her top dresser drawer. Although I knew I wasn't to rummage in these drawers, I took out the box sometimes to try to imagine these stones, some as big as the end of my thumb, in Mama's stomach behind the long scar from the operation. And sometimes I showed them to my friends for entertainment.

Pictures of Papa's parents hung on one side of the dresser. Although I never met my Grandfather Ott, it pleased me that my father looked so much like his father's picture.

*Orridine Beal, Dorotha
Beal Ott's mother.*

*Freeman Beal, Dorotha
Beal Ott's father.*

Mama's mother's picture hung on the other side of the
dresser. She looked ill, her thin face emphasizing the promi-
nent cheekbones of our Hart ancestors. A picture of her sister
Effie was there, too. When I asked Mama about that, she said
Aunt Effie was like a mother to her when her own mother
was in Wyoming with their brother, Emory, trying in vain to
regain her health. A picture of Mama's father sat on the little
desk in the kitchen, but I always wished there were one of
him on the bedroom wall with our other grandparents.

When I began to feel better, I got up a few minutes now
and then to practice on Mama's sewing machine, sitting in the
good light under the south window. I was determined to learn
to sew. Not too long before, Mama and I had visited her
friend Genie (Lucas) Downs, whose three daughters Lillian,
Lucille, and Irene were near my age. They were dressed alike
in red-checked gingham dresses trimmed at the neck with red
bias trim, which ended in the front with a bow. On the way
home I asked Mama, "Could I have a dress like those girls
were wearing?"

"Genie made those dresses. That's why they are so cute

and different. We wouldn't be able to buy one for you in a store."

"Could you make me one?"

When she told me she didn't believe she could copy them, I decided that some day I would learn to sew well enough to make clothes in the styles and colors I wanted. Ever after that I tried to sew, practicing at times as I did while I was recuperating. Mama taught me what she could, and I learned from school and 4-H. It wasn't a natural talent for me, and I had to work hard at it before I began to be satisfied with my efforts. It seemed so much more worthwhile than embroidering. This compulsion to sew was not a passing fancy. I sewed constantly until I retired (from teaching home economics).

Mama brought me a cool glass of water, felt my forehead, and asked how I felt. She always worried that one of my numerous illnesses would turn into tuberculosis, which had taken the lives of her mother and stepmother.

"I feel better. Can I look at the doctor book?"

She handed the book down to me from the top of the tall wardrobe where my parents' best clothes were kept. When I was very young, I took it down surreptitiously to look at when she was away from home. Now that I was older, she seemed to expect me to pore through it. The book had two sets of pictures with flaps that opened to reveal body parts. One showed the systems of the body (digestive, blood, and so on). The other set showed the human reproductive system, with the fetus in stages up to full term. Pages of colored plates showed plants that could be used in healing: belladonna, chicory, woundwort, arnica, and others. Could that book really have had children's stories in the back as it appears to me in my dreams?

Mama's hair, after she had it bobbed, also was stored on top of the wardrobe. We children enjoyed taking it down to run our fingers through its glossy length.

One piece of furniture in this room was new to us. Where the box that Mama had lovingly fixed to hold Dean's baby clothes had been was now a cedar chest bought from our neighbor, Mrs. Levine, before she moved. It was solid red cedar, with brass straps and studs like a buccaneer's treasure chest. One of Mrs. Levine's sons had made it for her. Mama liked it because it reminded her of this friend, as well as for its quality. The cedar chest is the only piece of furniture I now have from my parents' home. It is a treasured reminder of Mama and of a dear friend as well.

I have my own memories of this wren-like little lady from Sweden. Often I went over to borrow books belonging to the three Levine sons who lived at home — Westerns and romances of doubtful literary value — and my favorites, the Horatio Alger books. Mrs. Levine always asked me to stay and visit. I soon realized that she was not asking out of politeness but instead from loneliness, and I went over some evenings just to talk with her. She used Swedish words interspersed with her broken English. I soon caught on to the meaning ("Hon (he) went out to plow today"). I thought it was endearing. Several times when we were expecting company, Mama sent me over to borrow spoons. On my eleventh birthday, Mrs. Levine gave me six spoons of my own. I was touched by the gift and still have two of them after all of these years.

One summer evening I heard haunting music coming from their yard, and I started to go over. As I went closer, I saw that Mr. Levine was playing nostalgic tunes on his concertina. I thought he must be playing songs he remembered from Sweden. He played as if he were homesick, and it made me feel like crying. I didn't go into their yard, because I thought he was playing just for himself and his family. The family moved to an area of the country where other Swedish immigrants lived, and I hoped the Levines were happier there.

During all of the years we lived in this house, our baby crib, with metal bars like a circus cage, sat west of the bed. Although my younger brothers, Dale and Dean, used it in turn, I well remember lying in that crib waiting for sleep to overcome me. I could clearly hear a train that stopped in Greene each evening, less than two miles away as the sound waves flew. When it started up, I heard the wheels clickety-clack on the rails.

Mama had lived six years, from ages twelve to eighteen, in California, and she often told me about the mild weather and the beauty of the sea and the mountains. I knew that someday I must get on the train and go to California myself.

Therefore, the train wheels on the metal tracks called out to me, "Going to California, going to California," faster and faster, softer and softer, punctuated by the hoarse whistle, which warned as it approached a crossing. The words rushed together and whispered, "Going-to-California-going-to-California," and I slept.

THE CELLAR

Across from the sink, on the kitchen side of the cellar door, hung a roller towel, a narrow strip of natural linen with colored stripes on either edge. Mama made these towels from two-yard lengths of fabric flatfelled together at the ends. One end of the roller bar lifted up so the continuous length could be slipped over it. Pa's razor strop hung on this door until he began using a safety razor.

The cellar was small, being under only the kitchen and the south bedroom. To go down cellar, a person had to brush past the dishpans hung on nails against the west wall of the stairs. Draped over them was the dishrag, usually a piece of old underwear. Mama wouldn't waste money buying dish-cloths when we already had something that served the purpose just as well. I stayed close to this wall, not trusting the shaky railing along the inner side of the wooden steps. The last two steps were flat stones, turned toward the cellar.

Mama's home-canned food filled a wide shelf along the north wall. This shelf was an in area that had been excavated to waist height and covered with cement, as was the floor. Lined up on this shelf were hundreds of jars of home-canned food. Mama's eyes sparkled when she took a lamp down in the fall and inspected the rows and rows of food we had "put up" for the winter. The jars were carefully lined up so we knew almost by feel where to find each kind of food. Besides the fruits she bought and canned were jars of applesauce from our Dutchess and Wealthy apple trees, strawberries, rhubarb, and glasses of jams and jellies covered with paraffin. There were all kinds of pickles, including the crab apple ones I liked so well. From our garden were green beans, peas, tomatoes, and corn. All the work and sweat of the summer days were worth it, to have the family so well provided for. Many times in winter it was impossible to get to town. Having our own food squirreled away in the cellar was the best insurance against hunger. Most of what we canned kept very well, but once in awhile a winey smell alerted us to a jar of applesauce that had "worked," and we had to throw out the contents.

Also on the shelf were jars of canned beef and pork with juice jelled between the chunks of meat and a layer of hardened fat on the top. The day after butchering in the fall, all of us had to sit around the kitchen table to cut the fresh meat into chunks for canning. It was the most boring job imaginable, but we had to keep alert so we wouldn't cut ourselves with the knives Papa kept sharp by whisking them quickly up and down on the "steel." Mama packed the chunks of meat into canning jars, added a spoonful of salt to each, slipped the red rubber rings over the tops of the jars, and screwed the zinc lids in place. They were put into hot water in the copper boiler and boiled for hours. The smell of the rubber rings and the meat cooking made me feel ill, but I just had to bear it and keep on cutting up meat for the next cooker-full. After we had used a jar of meat, I had another unpleasant job. Slivers of meat clung firmly to the insides of the jars. For years my hands were small enough to fit into the jars and scour them out, whereas Mama's were too big. I knew I had to do it, but I detested the job.

It took a whole day in the fall for my parents to shred the cabbage for the twenty-gallon crock of sauerkraut we stored in the cellar each winter. They sat on the back porch and used a borrowed wooden hand shredder with metal blades to cut up the cabbage. Then they put a layer of cabbage into the crock and added a layer of salt. These layers were repeated until the crock was full. It was kept in a warm spot in the kitchen, between the stove and the sink, until it began the process of fermentation that turned it into sauerkraut. It was hard to believe that something that smelled so awful at this stage could turn out to taste so good. When it was ready, the heavy crock was carefully moved into the cellar and stored with a wooden cover held down by a clean rock. I never minded going down to dig out a serving dish of it with a fork, sampling the tangy shreds as I went. Except for canned fruit, it was our only winter salad, and we craved it, cold and juicy from the crock.

When she didn't have enough cucumbers at one time to make a batch of sweet or dill pickles, Mama mixed dry mustard with vinegar and salt and poured it into a smaller crock, putting in a few of the pickle-sized cucumbers. An inverted plate weighed down with an old flat iron kept the pickles immersed in liquid. Sour and crunchy, they were my favorite cucumber pickles. Toward the end of winter, as jars were available, she canned the last of the pickles. They tasted the same but kept better as the weather got warmer.

"Go down cellar and get some potatoes for supper," Mama often requested of me in late afternoon. "Bring up a jar of fruit — any kind you want — and a jar of meat."

I took a couple of stick matches from the tin dispenser in the kitchen and crept slowly down the steps, letting my eyes adjust to the darkness, and scratching a match on the stone wall. I hurriedly picked up the meat and a jar of peaches and put them on the steps. Then came the worse part — reaching into the potato bin along the east wall — especially in the spring, when the potatoes had grown sprouts curling out of each eye, like white larvae exposed when you pick up a rock. Even the second match I lit didn't provide enough light to distinguish the good from the bad, and my fingers often poked into a squishy, smelly, rotten part or gathered up a big dormant bug with the potato. Finally the pan would be full, and I would scurry upstairs.

"I'm scared to reach into that potato bin," I complained one day.

"That puts another star in your crown," Mama replied. She was always adding stars to people's heavenly crowns. "Besides, I don't like that job any better than you do."

I knew there was no way to shirk the miserable task.

Along the west wall of the cellar sat the bottom of an old trunk filled with sand, in which carrots were buried. It wasn't hard to dig these out, and they tasted so good. I begged Mama to let me eat them raw, but she said they were indigestible until they were cooked. I wish I could discuss that with her now.

High on the east and south walls were short windows that let in light and air when they were opened. In the winter they were covered with the straw Papa banked around the foundation to keep the house warmer. Then all the light available was from the door to the kitchen, when it was open. The flue from the kitchen stove was grounded in the center of the cellar, a square pillar of brick, cobwebby and dusty, cutting off light that might have come into dark corners of the cellar.

On the floor at the center of the south wall was a hole broken out of the cement floor, with round orange tiles sloping downward out of it. Here the water from the kitchen sink ran on its way to its destination, the ditch south of the driveway. Some water always stood in the hole, exuding a musty smell. Because of this primitive arrangement, we could pour only clear water down the sink—no greasy dishwater or coffee grounds. Nevertheless, we were proud to have running water and a working sink in our house. Some farmers' wives had to carry water into the house in a pail, and out the same way.

When a cyclone threatened, we took refuge in the southeast corner of the cellar, believed to be the safest place if the roof were to be blown off over our heads. One summer we had so many scares that Mama put chairs down there in an attempt to make it a bit more comfortable. Usually, though, the winds lasted only a short time. When it sounded quieter, and especially when it started to rain, Pa walked up a step or two of the outside stairway and cautiously lifted up the slanted door to take a look. We never had any serious damage, but places around us often lost a barn, trees, or even a house, sucked up by the whirlwind fury of the wind.

In the nice summer weather, Mama opened the windows and laid back the outside doors to air the cellar. With this air and light shining in, it was not the gloomy place it seemed in the winter. I liked having a cellar with the old-fashioned slanting doors, and sang to myself a children's song that ended,

> Shout down my rain barrel,
> Slide down my cellar door . . .
> And we'll be jolly friends,
> Forevermore.

Isolated from girls my age as I usually was, I daydreamed of having a friend who would come over to slide down my cellar door and be my jolly friend, even though it might not be forevermore.

2

Family Life

Robert Ott, one year old;
the family house is in the background.

A SMALL GIRL WONDERS

In the hot, dusty August the milk soured quickly and the flies buzzed around, heedless of the spirals of sticky flypaper hanging from the ceiling. My brother Robert scooted around on the floor, not quite ready to walk. I liked to get down on the floor and play peek-a-boo with him to make him laugh.

One day he was feverish and listless and refused to play. The doctor came at noon and took medicine for Robert out of his little black bag. He diagnosed the illness as cholera infantum, a dread disease that took the lives of many infants in households with no refrigeration.

"Isn't there something, anything we can do?" my parents pleaded to the doctor as Robert grew worse. And so Dr. Bigelow asked the specialist to make the long trip from Waterloo. This specialist, Dr. Waterbury, gently told my parents that it was too late for him to help.

Robert lay uncomplaining, obediently swallowing the useless doses of medicine.

I remember that Harry and I were playing boisterously under the young elm tree when someone asked us to play more quietly out of respect for our brother, who had just died.

Later, a man I didn't know spent a long time behind the closed door of the parlor. Curious, I went in when no one was around. Robert lay on a bench with red cloths on his face. He lay so still. I peeked under the cloth. Why wouldn't he open his eyes and play our game? Why wouldn't he laugh for me? I went to Mama and asked her about the red cloths. She said the man wanted to make Robert's cheeks look pink and healthy.

Friends and neighbors brought fragrant flowers from their gardens, and they sat in rows on borrowed chairs in the parlor. Before them Robert slept in a soft white bed, cheeks rosier than in life. He held a pink rosebud in one hand and wore the crisp, white rompers Mama had finished only the week before. While the preacher talked, the family sat secluded in the small bedroom that opened off the parlor. Mama held her handkerchief to her face and sobbed softly. Tears slipped down Papa's cheeks. I was surprised, because I thought a man would never cry. Aunt Jen sat with us, too, and looked sad.

Then we were all moving around and getting into cars. I rode in an open car, in the back seat with Aunt Jen. Between us and the front seat was a seat that folded down. On this was what looked to me like a small white mattress, rolled up. Aunt Jen, looking stern, just shook her head when I asked about it. Someone told me that Robert was in the "mattress." Where was his pretty bed? It was all so hard to understand.

It was many years before I realized that caskets have no legs; they rest upon a stand. Then at last I understood that why had appeared to my four-year-old eyes to be a mattress was in reality a closed, tufted casket lifted off the stand it sat on in the parlor.

THE BARNSTORMER

One cool October Saturday evening after we had delivered our eggs to be candled and had gone inside so Mama could give her order, the clerk said, "Did you hear about the big train wreck at Clarksville? We're hearing all kinds of reports about it. Sounds like several were injured."

As we went out in front of the store, we joined a knot of

ladies discussing the wreck: "Two railroad cars turned over. I heard some people were hurt bad."

Mama entered the conversation. "I just heard about it. What caused it?"

"I don't know, but several people were hurt, and luggage is strewed all over," offered someone else. "Wouldn't it be a sight to see?"

I stayed close to Mama, half frightened by the discussion. We crossed the street to go to the drug store.

The men, in clean bib overalls and blue chambray work shirts, lounged as usual against the storefronts on this side of Main Street and discussed the wreck. I caught fragments of their conversations as we passed. "They say one car turned clear over—blood all over the place. Might be worth the trip."

Sunday was a crisp, fall day, just begging for an outing, and the wreck was as good an excuse as any. So Pa decided we could go; Aunt Jen and Grandpa went along. The ladies wore their stylish big-brimmed velvet hats, secured through their braids with long hat pins. I listened to them visit amiably as we sped along the rutted dirt roads, so much faster than old Bess and the buggy. For me the twenty-two mile ride in the open touring car was almost fun enough.

We must have seen the wreck and thrilled vicariously to the danger that had been, but I have no recollection of it. I do remember the festive feeling as we gathered sociably in the sunny air, talking with others we knew.

"I brought a little lunch along. It's enough to share, if you'd like to join us," Mama invited.

"I have some things along, too," answered a friend. "Let's put it together. It'll be more fun that way."

Mama brought out the lunch that we had hurriedly put together after church. We had minced ham sandwiches, cookies, and tangy-sweet applesauce from our Wealthy tree. Several others joined us. No other children were there, so I helped Mama.

The women put the food on tablecloths laid out on the ground. We sat on folded-up blankets brought along for this purpose, or on rocks or logs.

"We decided we might as well make a day of it," the women agreed. "We won't have many more pleasant days like this before it snows."

The real excitement of the day was the presence of an airplane in a pasture nearby—the first one Harry and I had ever seen so close. Mama told me, in answer to my questions, that the pilot was a barnstormer, there to make a little money by offering rides to the crowd.

Papa parked the car in a wooded area, and we walked through the brush and prickly stubble to get closer. It was hard to believe that this contraption, looking like a huge box kite, could actually rise from the ground at the will of its pilot, soar majestically through the sky, and float down to the ground.

A few brave souls paid their money and, with a show of bravado, put their lives in the hands of the pilot and God. Landing safely in due time, they stepped down with proud smiles. I clapped with the watching crowd, seeing these daring persons as bigger than life.

To encourage more riders, the daredevil pilot, a dashing figure in his helmet and goggles, gave an exhibition of stunt flying, doing loops, nose dives, and other scary tricks. No one walked on a wing as we had seen done at the fair, but the performance was sufficiently exciting for us.

Harry and I looked on in awe. When we heard the sound of a plane flying over our house, we always ran out to see it. We'd never seen one this close.

"Would you go up if you could?" I asked Harry. "I would."

"You bet I would, in a minute," he answered quickly.

No matter how we might long to go, we knew we had no chance. It cost a lot of money, and our parents would think it foolish to waste it on such a venture. We were glad we could just watch and be a part of the crowd.

"I liked seeing the plane fly better than I liked the train wreck," I said on the way home.

"I think we all did," answered Pa. "That was something to make a person think."

THE H'RD GIRL

I t was between the war to end war and the Great Depression. "Silent Cal" Coolidge was President, and times were good. Even my frugal parents thought they could afford occasional household help, a "h'rd" girl (which is what "hired girl" sounded like in Papa's Pennsylvania accent).

Ruth Rodman had helped us several times but was busy at another job this time when Mama called. "My sister, Elsie, could help if you'd like," Ruth suggested. "She's younger, but she'd be good help, and she wants the work." Girls who had finished school and were not yet married had few other work options. "Hiring out" was a respectable occupation.

Elsie was very young and saucy, with a real zest for living. She washed the cream separator, with its tedious, sharp little discs, with as much gusto as she swept the kitchen floor. Her evenings were free, and often a ruddy-faced young man with warm brown eyes came to take her out. He would sit on the edge of his chair, turning and turning his straw boater in his hands as he waited for Elsie to appear. Then she would bounce down the stairs, fragrant with lilac talc, wearing a bright dress to set off her marcelled black hair. She would take him in arm, and off they would go.

After an evening out, Elsie seemed to have a special glow and would fill the kerosene lamps and wash their sooty chimneys with a song on her lips. I especially remember one, which went:

> I loved her in the springtime,
> I loved her in the fall,
> But last night, on the back porch,
> I loved her best of all.

This was the first popular song I became familiar with, and I listened with pleasure to the cheery voice singing it over and over. Mama also smiled and never chided at what must have been an interminable repetition.

Papa liked to pretend he was falling for Elsie, with her flirty ways. Once he even brought her a little striped paper sack of candy from town and made of it an occasion for teasing Mama. "Well, Dorothy, I guess you'd better watch out while Elsie's around, for you're apt to lose me." The words were belied by the look of love in Papa's eyes as he glanced at Mama, the answering twinkle in her eyes, and her Mona Lisa smile. I could see that he was only joking and felt warm and secure to be a part of this loving family. I wanted Elsie to stay with us always for bringing such fun to our usually staid household.

I remember little else about Elsie, but at odd times, even today, I remember, "Last night, on the back porch," and smile.

WAIT UNTIL MAY 18

It was one of those unseasonably warm days that sometimes come in early spring to beguile us into believing that the tiresome winter has finally gone. We pupils of Pleasant Grove #8 burst out of the shadowy, chalk-scented schoolhouse into the bright sun and clean air and stood a moment to let our eyes adjust to the change. We felt renewed and vigorous as we breathed in the balmy air and started on our various ways home.

Coats were too warm to wear, so Harry and I carried ours as we loitered along the mile road home. Water trickled in the ditches, and buds burgeoned in the long lane of trees on either side of the road. Birds that had wintered over announced their joy at finding new green shoots to eat, as did insects awakened from their dormant winter. Pussy willow buds partly hidden by their green coats seemed almost ready to burst forth in their fluffy gray gowns. Surely this warm air, these signs of spring called to my brother and me for some expression suitable to this spring fever weather!

Harry suggested, "Let's go barefoot!" It took only a moment to take off our heavy shoes, unhook the long, lisle stockings from our pantywaists, and slide them off our feet. We happily squished our tender toes through the soft dirt where the muddy ruts had dried. We didn't notice the patches of ice that still lay frozen in the leaves where the shade was heavy. I forgot my painful earaches and chilblains of the winter. We were completely blissful.

As we neared home, we could hear the Plymouth Rocks cluck their joy at being out of the confining hen house. All the farm sounds seemed crystal clear to my acute senses.

We stopped to play with the barn kittens as they frolicked in the sun. Their staid mamas awoke at the sound of our excited voices and, stretching luxuriously, came toward us to be petted.

Papa rode in from the field on the noisy disc, behind old Topsy and Bess.

"Isn't it nice, Papa?" I greeted him. "It's warm, like summer weather."

Papa smiled until he saw the shoes in our hands, and our bare feet. "What in tarnation do you two think you're doing, going barefoot in April? You'll catch your death of cold," he reproached us, his face stern.

In dismay, Harry and I looked at each other. For the first time we began to realize we had done something foolish. Pa pulled the long horsewhip out of its socket on the disk and swept its fringed end across our bare legs. "Don't let me see you barefoot again until it's warm enough. Now get up to the house." Papa had whipped us! I couldn't believe it!

With long faces we raced to the house and Mama. Seeing tears on my face, and Harry frowning as he tried not to cry, she looked alarmed and asked, "What happened? Are you hurt?"

"Pa whipped us because we went barefoot," I informed her, "but we didn't mean to be naughty."

"He didn't really whip us," Harry said. "He just swished the end of the whip across our legs."

Having ascertained that no real harm had been done to feelings or to feet, she agreed with Papa. Even though the air was warm, the ground was cold. We'd have to wait awhile to cast off winter clothing. She opened down the oven door and said, "Pull up your chairs and warm your feet. Then put on your shoes and stockings again."

Beginning to free ourselves from the enormity of our guilt, we asked, "But when can we go barefoot?"

Then Mama told us that when she was little, she and her brothers were allowed to go barefoot after May 18, her brother Burton's birthday. That solved the problem fairly. Henceforth we were guided every spring by this rule, and we looked forward to Uncle Burton's birthday and the freedom to go barefoot.

Dorotha Ott and Uncle Burton.

MY BROTHER DALE

I t was strange and annoying the way my feet kept bumping into the bars on the end of my crib that July morning, two weeks before I turned five. When I roused, I realized I was on the front porch couch. Harry was on the other end, and our feet were touching. Mystified, I went into the kitchen, and the lady who was there fixing breakfast told me I had a new baby brother. I had been moved out of my parents' room in the night so I wouldn't be disturbed. Mama was resting, but the lady showed me the red-faced new baby, sleeping in his basket. It was interesting but not earth-shaking.

Just a few weeks before, Mama had washed a big load of baby clothes and hung them to dry in the sunshine. I wondered why she did this, and she said she just wanted everything clean. For several days after the baby was born, when anyone came to see him, I would say, "Isn't it lucky that Mama washed all the baby clothes two weeks ago?" Mama and the ladies would smile and agree with me.

When Dale was about six months old, we had a family picture taken, in three sections. In one of the panels, Harry stood beside Mama; I, in another, with a big bow clipped to my hair, was with Papa; and in the middle section, Dale was pictured alone. He wore a dress, as both boys and girls did then for most of their first year. Mama had made the white dress, though a friend had made the inserts and trim of tatting. Dale looked good-natured and amiable in that picture, as he does today.

One day when Dale was two, Mama and I came back to the house from the garden and couldn't find him. He had been playing contentedly with his blocks and little wagon when we left the house a few moments before. After a quick search of the house, Mama's first thought was of the stock tank in the barnyard. We rushed across the dusty, rutted yard, with Mama muttering prayerfully, "Oh, no, he couldn't have opened the gate—climbed the fence—no, he couldn't have fallen into the tank—oh, no!" With relief, we did not find him drowned in the stock tank.

Calling, "Dale, Dale, where are you? Answer me, Dale!" we made a circuit of the farm buildings, with no luck. Surely he couldn't have wandered into the cornfield, where a youngster could be lost for days in the tall corn! We ran back to the house, and Mama frantically called the neighbor across the road to help in the search. They were nearly ready to call Pa in from the field when the object of our search rolled out from under the Hoosier kitchen cabinet. He had laid down there for a nap, completely hidden, and now he looked from one to the other of us as if he wondered why we were all staring at him with such pleasure. Mama gave him a big hug, and he hugged her, too. "H'wo, Mama," he said, and he smiled cheerfully at the rest of us.

One evening when Dale was four, he was sitting with our parents and Harry and me on the sparse grass by the windmill, cooling off after the hot day. I was listening with interest to the discussion of our planned trip to the State Fair. The boys were cavorting around in high spirits. Harry turned a somersault, and his feet struck Dale's left arm. It wasn't a particularly hard hit. Dale had survived worse. But he was on all fours and his arms were braced. He cried, as much in surprise as in pain, and ran to Mama to be comforted. Pa didn't scold, because he had seen the whole thing and realized that no harm had been intended.

It was obvious the arm was broken. It had a strange twist to it just below the elbow. Mama called Dr. Bigelow, and he said to meet him at his office. After examining the arm, he said he would have to give Dale an anesthetic while he set it.

When Dale woke up, he said, "It seems like I wasn't here for awhile." I thought he was pretty smart to figure this out and express it so well.

The doctor explained that this was a "greenstick" frac-

orotha and Harry Ott.   *Dale Ott.*   *Margaret and Paul Ott.*

ture, not a complete break as it might have been in an older person. Mama was careful to get instructions for care of the splinted arm: "Just be sure the bandage stays dry. The arm will hurt less if he keeps it in the sling. Bring him back in three weeks, sooner if he has any trouble with it." Then Mama mentioned the State Fair trip and said she supposed we'd better not go. Dr. Bigelow said the broken arm needn't prevent us from going unless some unforeseen complication were to occur before that time. Harry was looking very upset. Mama assured him that the accident was not his fault and that Dale would be all right. I remember thinking that now I'd always know what a broken arm looked like. And, yes, we did go to the State Fair.

On an October evening when Dale was ten, he came home from Ramkers' complaining of a headache. This was unusual enough for Mama to check into. Dale said he thought he got into too much smoke from the leaf bonfire he and Jerry had made. After a restless night, he woke up with a high fever. Mama mentally went through her repertoire of children's diseases. She opened his pajama top and saw a red rash on his chest. She suspected scarlet fever, a frightening disease she suffered through as a child.

The doctor came out, confirmed the diagnosis, and instructed Mama in caring for the sick boy. He explained that the Health Officer would have to put a quarantine sign on our door. No one could come to see us, and those quarantined could not leave the farm. Cream and eggs could not be sold, which was a blow to our family economy.

Harry was sent to town to stay with Aunt Jen so he could attend school, but I was quarantined. I was not sick, so I enjoyed the enforced vacation. I took long walks on the farm, dreaming my way through the autumn haze, watching the spiders spinning their gossamer webs, observing the busy ants and the squirrels.

Every evening I watched the men unload the wagons of handpicked corn into the elevator, which carried it up into the corncrib. Radio was interesting, and I listened to the great Minnesota football game each weekend. All this grew tiresome, finally, and I began to worry how I would ever make up all the schoolwork I had missed.

After the number of weeks required for our quarantine had passed, we had to fumigate the house. For a whole day, cones of formaldehyde had to be burned in the tightly sealed house. Then Mama took Dale, Dean, and me to shop in Charles City. We ate lunch in a restaurant and were surprised at how much of the day was left after this unusual treat. We rode around awhile to see the bright colors of the leaves, but that didn't take long. I should have enjoyed this chance to ride around when it was so pretty outside, but killing time when everyone else was in school didn't feel right. At last we stopped to open the house to air it. For an hour we visited at Ramkers'. Then we went home to a thoroughly chilled house. That odious smell permeated everything and lingered many weeks. All rules having been complied with, Papa took down the hateful sign and we were no longer pariahs.

For the next several years Dale suffered with legaches. The doctor had no explanation; he just said they must be "growing pains." Mama wasn't satisfied with this, but one didn't disagree with a doctor and Dale had to bear the pain as best he could. A number of tests would be run on today's child, and some diagnosis made. Dale apparently had no lasting effects.

After this, Dale gained weight and even became a bit pudgy. Papa began to call him "Stubbie" or "Stub," and others of us took up the nickname. Dale wasn't pleased with it, but he was too agreeable to fuss. Later, when he was transferred to a different country school after ours closed, he told me the kids there called him "The Old Gray Otter," derived from Ott, our last name. I felt a little hurt by this and asked, "Are they making fun of you?"

"No," he responded, "I think it means they like me."

HER CROWNING GLORY

Mama was proud of her long, lustrous hair, worn in a bun on the back of her head. Usually she would twist the luxuriant mass of it into a rope, and then, pulling it up, make a coil of it all. A few bone hairpins would secure it, and she would tuck the ends under, maybe putting in another pin or two. This quick arrangement would last all day. She never pulled it starkly back into the bun. Instead, it seemed soft around her face. This softness was enhanced when feminine tendrils escaped during the day and curled around her face and in the nape of her neck.

At bedtime she would pull out the pins and let her hair cascade sensuously down her back. It would snap and crackle with electricity as she brushed the dark brown length of it, chestnut lights glowing in its sheen.

Then she would plait it into two thick braids. I learned to braid by watching her quick hands perform this nightly task. I marveled at the deft way she could wrap the ends of

Dorotha Beal Ott at age four.

each braid with some long strands pulled from her brush, fixing it securely for the night.

Mama was a bit vain about her hair, telling me that she was glad it was thick enough to make two fat braids, not skimpy ones, "like some have."

In the morning she would run her fingers through the twists of the braids, to separate them, and comb through them to make her hair smooth. Then up it would go for the day, the whole process taking only a few minutes.

In the 1920s women were being emancipated by getting their hair cut. It was a traumatic decision—to bob or not to bob. One wanted to be up-to-date, but that hair had been growing all the years of a woman's life. "Putting her hair up" was symbolic of becoming an adult.

Mama and her friend, Helen Lucas, had talked often and long on the subject. "Having short hair would have some advantages," Mama said. "Think how easy it would be to wash and dry."

"Do you suppose we'd look like Clara Bow?" Helen asked. She always seemed to make a little joke when a discussion got serious.

"The trouble is, once it's cut, we can't change our minds," Mama mused.

"Don't worry about that, Dorothy. It will grow out again."

Decisions were made and revoked, but progress was inevitable, and the deed must be done. The date was finally set. Helen and Percy and their child, Genevieve, came to our farm home one balmy summer evening.

"You women may look like a couple of strangers when you get home. What do you think, Perce? Should we let them go through with it?" teased Papa.

"They seem to have their minds made up," answered Percy. "I guess we can get used to it."

"What do you really think, Paul?" asked Mama apprehensively. "Shall we think it over a couple more weeks?"

"You do just what you want to do. You don't need our permission."

I thought maybe Mama and Helen wanted the men to tell them what to do, but the men wouldn't. So, giving each other courage, Mama and Helen set off in our open car for the barbershop. It was not made easier by the knowledge that they were going into a man's domain, with its spittoons and its pool hall in the back room.

Papa and Percy occupied their time by freezing the ice cream Mama had mixed up before she left. Percy had stopped at the icehouse beside the river and bought a sawdust-covered block of ice. After rinsing off the sawdust at the well, Pa put the ice in a gunnysack and crushed it with a few blows from the side of the ax. He fitted the metal cylinder, with its cream and egg mixture, into the center of the wooden tub. Next came the crosspiece connecting the dasher to the crank. Taking turns, he and Percy turned the crank until the difficulty of turning indicated that the cream was frozen. When the cork was pulled from the hole in the side of the freezer, ice water and salt gushed out. The dasher, dripping with icy goodness, was handed to the nearest child. Harry and I knew enough to have spoons and tongues ready for this messy treat. Pa plugged the hole in the center with a rag, repacked the tub with ice and salt, and covered it with more gunnysacks. Then it was left to ripen for the celebration.

In due time the women came home. Shyly, almost fearfully, each carrying her cut-off hair wrapped in a paper, they got out of the car and came over to the waiting ones who sat on the cement porch. "How do we look? Is it OK?" they asked, turning gracefully before us.

Dale, who was just a toddler, had to be held and comforted and reassured that this was indeed his Mama. My stomach felt funny, and I wasn't sure if I liked the short hair. Harry just grinned.

Pa said, "You look mighty fine."

Percy commented, "Paul, we've got ourselves a couple of flappers for sure."

Then, in that dusky evening, came a breathless moment when time hung suspended. We faced the present with a wistful look back. Were we ready for life's changes and the course that lay ahead? In that moment I caught a glimpse into my future and realized that life would always present changes. I knew I wanted to face these challenges unafraid, to go forward, not to cling to old ways for security.

Harry asked, "When is that ice cream going to be ready?" and we breathed again. Mama went in for spoons and dishes, and served us all. The ladies flipped their heads around to enjoy the new sensation, and they talked in low tones about what was still uppermost in their minds.

"Maybe I'll just turn the ends under with a curling iron or have a marcel for a special day. Well, it's done now, that's for sure."

By the time the ice cream was gone, my stomach felt fine, and I was proud of my modern mother.

Mama could have sold her hair for quite a sum, for use in making wigs, but she kept it for possible use in a "switch" for herself at some time. It was kept in a shoe box on the top

Dorotha and Harry Ott; be-   *Helen and Genevieve Lucas;*
fore "the bob." ⟷ *also before "the bob."*

of the tall wardrobe in her bedroom, and I enjoyed taking it
down to look at it. It never lost its beauty, though we kept it
until after her death. Then it was suitably disposed of, and
she was truly gone.

OUR NEW BABY

I was in the fifth grade when Mama, that May, said she guessed she wouldn't run in the races the last day of school. I had always been so proud to have her enter into the games and races after the picnic. At thirty-three, she was the youngest of the mothers. She seemed like a different person as she put aside her usual decorum and ran nimbly in the races, carefree as she seldom appeared in her role as a mother.

I was disappointed and asked, "Why not?"

"It's because of the baby sister you're going to get," she replied.

A wave of emotions swept over me. I was astonished, pleased, and embarrassed all at once. Mama waited for my response to this astounding piece of news. She knew (I'd told her often enough) that my heart's desire was to have a baby sister. My mind raced over the implications.

Finally I gasped, "Does Pa know?"

She answered seriously, "Yes, I think he knows."

I asked how she knew it would be a girl, and when she would be born.

"It won't be until the end of summer," she responded, "and I just have a feeling it will be a girl."

I realize now that because she had borne four boys and only one girl, she would be likely to think that she would have a girl.

What was for a short while our secret was soon known by all, and Mama's friends rejoiced with us. I was slightly embarrassed at her enlarging figure, but proud, too.

She needed new dresses to fit, and Mama and I especially liked the one we called her "red-and-green-pepper" dress because of the figures in the small print.

There were baby clothes to be made, so Mama bought

yards and yards of white outing flannel. She made soft little kimonos and receiving blankets, trimming them with her beautiful hand embroidery: chain stitch and feather stitch, with a French knot here and there.

I was just beginning to develop my obsession with sewing, and Mama taught me how to make a narrow hem. Hemming diaper after diaper was good practice. When I wasn't satisfied with my sewing, Mama said it didn't have to be perfectly even.

One afternoon I came into the house and found Mama in her bedroom, tacking cloth to the outside of a square wooden box. She said she was fixing the box to hold the clothes we had been getting ready for the new baby. Papa had put casters on the bottom four corners of the box and attached the lid at the back with hinges. The inside was painted white, and the lid was padded and covered with a pretty, blue-flowered cretonne. Mama was just finishing tacking pleats of cretonne on the front and sides. I watched as she worked on the box, and I remember so clearly the happy, fulfilled look on her face.

In 1928 babies were born at home, and Mama had many necessary preparations to make for her confinement. It was all a big puzzle to me, but she wore that happy, bemused look on her face, and it was something special to see. One day she washed a beautiful embroidered nightgown that I had never seen. She said she kept it for "good," for when she might be sick and have to stay in bed. Only as I write this do I realize that I have always kept a good nightgown in reserve, in case I'd be sick in bed. Such small events can have such lasting effects in our lives.

That summer is a shining memory in my life. It made me feel grown-up to help and to share a special happiness and age-old feelings with Mama.

One September morning before daylight, I heard comings and goings downstairs. When I got up, a practical nurse was fixing breakfast, but there was no baby sister. The doctor had come and gone, having decided he would not be needed for some hours yet. Papa looked worried. Harry had arrived before the doctor did, and Pa didn't want to have that experience again.

After school Harry, Dale, and I hurried home and entered a house smelling of Lysol. We were a little hesitant about entering the bedroom, but the nurse who was in the kitchen said, "I think your mother has something to show you," and she preceded us into the bedroom.

We found a smiling mother in her bed, and the nurse held up a beautiful baby for us to see.

Mama stopped smiling and said, uncertainly, "It's a boy, Margaret."

I replied at once, "I wouldn't trade him for a thousand girls!"

And I still wouldn't.

The next morning the nurse sat in a chair in front of the open oven door, bathing the red-faced baby. I was amazed at the proportions of a newborn baby's body. His head seemed so big for the little body, and his scrawny legs weren't much bigger than Papa's fingers. He had hardly any chin at all. When the tight wool band around his stomach was taken off, the tied end of the cord was repulsive looking. Though he weighed nine and one-half pounds, he seemed so tiny. Still, there was never a more beautiful baby.

The nurse asked me to bring her the thermometer so she could check Mama's temperature. I felt important to be asked. Wanting to be a good helper, I took the steaming teakettle off the cookstove, went to the sink, and poured the boiling water over the thermometer to sterilize it. As I saw the glass tube shatter and the mercury puddling in the sink, I realized too late that 212-degree water should not be poured over a thermometer that reads only to 110 degrees. I felt so bad that I really didn't need the gentle reprimand I got.

Because this baby was not "Barbara" after all, we had to choose a boy's name. It took a few days of thought.

Upon hearing from me that the baby still had no name, neighbor Louis Ramker said, "How about . . . ?" and he recited several nice names, including Merlin and Dean.

As I hurried home to share these suggestions, I saw Pa

out by the hog house talking to a friend who had stopped by to congratulate him. Papa's face wore such a proud look, just as if this were his firstborn son. As he threw corn to the hogs, he considered my list of names. By the next day we'd all agreed on "Dean Merlin," and I knew I'd had a real part in naming my brother.

From the very first, I rocked him, changed his diapers, and carried him around wherever we went. Mama was especially glad for my help during Dean's late afternoon fussy spell.

Soon he was old enough to welcome me home from

Dean Ott, six years old,
standing in the outside cellar door.

school with crows of delight and wildly waving arms and legs. I was thrilled to be so warmly greeted. We played all the baby games together: Pat-a-Cake, This Little Piggy Went to Market, Peek-a-Boo, and a few of our own invention.

I remember holding Dean on my lap as we rode to town one afternoon. He was asleep, and his little mouth was working as if he were nursing. I told Mama about it. "Do you think he's dreaming?" I asked.

"He can't tell us, but I suppose he is," she said. "What kind of dreams do you suppose a baby has?"

The next summer Deon Ramker, who was a few years younger than I and lived nearby, in the house where I was born, played dolls with me, but my doll was really alive. I wheeled him between her house and mine in my big doll buggy, and Dean was glad for the outings.

Dean was a handsome child, with big brown eyes and very blond hair. Mama said, "I always wanted a child with beautiful brown eyes like your Pa." I was proud to show off my little brother at church and in town.

From the time he was a year old, he'd stand with his back to my legs, and I'd pick him up and swing him onto my shoulders. He was completely trusting and liked the view from that vantage point. He also liked to stand on a chair or tabletop and leap into my waiting arms. Once he launched himself off the fourth step going upstairs, and I hadn't expected him to. I barely caught him. I began to realize what a responsibility it was to have the care of a child.

HARRY AND MERRYLEGS

My brother, Harry, a year older than I, has unflaggingly loved horses since his earliest years. We often played a game of stick horses, with branches from the old grove north of the house. A sturdy branch was a work horse, whereas a slender stick became to us a beautiful riding horse. We stabled these horses in the pales of the wire fence around the grove and gave them the best of care. The knots along the wood became insect galls, which we treated with salve from little, round, tin sample boxes that came in the mail. We would gallop astride our horses to imaginary destinations and home again, pawing dirt realistically with our bare feet. No Arabians could have seemed finer.

Harry yearned for a pony like a town boy might hope for a bicycle. When Daiker's grocery store held a contest with a small pony as a prize, Harry dreamed of winning her. Mama discouraged such hopes, knowing disappointment would likely be the result. Then the owner of Daiker's asked us to pasture the pony through the summer weeks of the contest. Harry delightedly rode around the farm and the neighborhood, making sure his charge had ample exercise. Little though the pony was, she was just right for the boy who rode her. No one spoke of it the day the winner was to be chosen. In the late afternoon the telephone call came, and Harry had not won. When he saw the winner ride off on his prize, Harry walked away toward the barn with a set face and a blurry look in his eyes. At supper time he shrugged off Mama's questioning look and wouldn't talk to any of us.

One morning the next spring Pa said, "Harry, we'd better get going to that sale. Cecil, you come along, too." Cecil was our hired man. As they left, Mama and Papa exchanged a conspiratorial glance.

After they had gone, Mama confided to me, "Papa knows a man who has ponies for sale, and he's going to see if he can buy one. Harry doesn't know about it."

When they came home, Harry raced into the house with Pa not far behind. Both wore big grins. "W-we bought a Shetland pony. She's just a colt. H-her name is Merrylegs, and her mother is Blackbird. Cecil is riding her home." Harry stuttered in excitement. "She-she's brown, and she's the best one of the lot."

When Cecil rode her into the yard, we hurried out to see her. Merrylegs was not fully grown, but she looked big to me, because I was used to the little pony. She was all brown with soft brown eyes. I knew at once that was exactly what a pony should look like.

"Want to ride her, Skeeter?" Pa asked me. (He called me "Skeeter," short for mosquito, because I was so small for my age.) He lifted me up on her back. I didn't know how to make her go, so I just held the reins and looked at the world from this new perspective. Papa slapped her rump and she took a few steps. It was a little scary, and I clung to her mane, sure I was going to fall off. Harry was waiting, so I slid off to the ground. I needed time to think about riding her.

This pony was ours to keep, so we dared to fall in love with her. She was a young pony with a gentle temperament. She never balked or refused to obey. We rode her bareback, with only a bridle to control her. A few clucks of the tongue or a light swat of the open hand on her rump was enough to get her to do our bidding. Harry lavished care upon her. He loved her and fed her, curried her, and rode her whenever he could.

We rode her double to school, when the weather was nice, tethering her to the flagpole. She stood patiently, eating the plentiful grass, swishing her tail and stamping her hooves to rid herself of the pesky flies. We were the envy of our schoolmates.

Papa had a little wooden spring wagon built, just Merrylegs' size. Wearing a pony-sized set of harness, she was ready to work. Several times that summer Harry and I harnessed

Aunt Edna, Dale, Harry, and Margaret
admiring Merrylegs.

her, filled the wagon with sweet corn, drove the two miles to town, and sold the corn door to door. Housewives were pleased to get the fresh sweet corn for ten cents a dozen ears from such a pleasant young salesman. I sat in the wagon and drove as Harry went down the street. Our wagon emptied quickly.

On our way home from one such trip, we met a friend of my parents. I was afraid of the man because I had heard he was a bachelor, and I didn't know what that word meant. I was too shy to speak to him and shut my eyes as we met. Harry was so angry at me for my rudeness that he pushed me off the seat onto the metal rim of the turning wagon wheel. My right leg was gashed just below the knee, and the scar is visible to this day.

Merrylegs once carried us north past the schoolhouse, toward the woods where Papa bought wood each fall to fell, cut, and split for our heating stove. I had never ridden so far from home, but Harry always dared to go farther than I. Before we got to the woods, we glimpsed a short, white-haired boy sitting by himself in a pasture. He jumped up eagerly and grinned at our approach. He explained that he was in charge of the herd of cattle grazing in the lush pasture, which his father had rented for the summer. It was important work, but boring, and he seemed glad for the company. Ralph, for that was his name, was just Harry's age. He asked us to come back. Harry must have found other times to slip away from his tasks, as the boys became lifelong friends.

Early one Christmas morning when we were examining our presents, Papa told Harry to get some cobs for the kitchen cookstove. Harry, upset anyway by the paucity of his gifts, glowered. In a gruff voice Pa ordered him to "get those cobs." Harry started out to the cob house. In seconds he was back, wearing a wide grin, almost too excited to tell us of the discovery he had made on the back porch. He had found the best gift of all, a small, green, wooden sled for Merrylegs to pull. It was hard to tell who was the most pleased—Harry or the parents who watched his delight. I couldn't see why a dumb old sled was so special. I thought my new doll was a much better gift, but no one made a fuss over her.

I spent many happy summer hours riding Merrylegs bareback. When my few morning chores were done, I would go, bridle in hand, to the barnyard. There she stood with the horses, head drooping, as if waiting for some fun in her life. She patiently took the bit in her mouth and let me put the bridle over her ears and fasten it. I'd lead her through the gate and throw the reins over her head. I grasped her mane and gave a big jump. This landed me jackknifed across her back, head on one side and legs on the other. A scramble worked my legs astride her broad back. I wouldn't have won any points for style, but Merrylegs and I were satisfied with the results. Unhampered by further restraints, we would ride out in the fresh morning air.

Most often we would begin our adventure by turning north through the trees. I liked to ride to the west side of the school yard, where the orange lilies bloomed. These exotic looking flowers never bloomed while school was open, spring or fall, but only in the summer months. Then the schoolhouse hid them from the view of passersby. I believed I was the only person who saw them and wondered why summer-blooming flowers had been planted in this hidden spot.

If there was plenty of time, we'd go around the dirt road of the sparsely settled section square, a ride of four miles. The willing pony obeyed my every whim as I daydreamed the miles away. Sometimes I urged Merrylegs on to her easy gallop for a short while, gently pushing my heels into her soft stomach. I was an untrained rider, my arms flapping awkwardly as I rode, but I was happy in my simplicity. Most often we meandered along, she nipping a bite of grass now and then from the side of the road. If she caught me unaware, I had to grab her mane to keep from sliding over her head. Birds sang us on our way as we passed. Redwing blackbirds in the slough swooped from stalk to stalk, calling out their hoarse "okalee, okalee." Meadowlarks on fenceposts or swaying on a strand of barbed wire lilted their complex syllables over and over. The crops grew day by day, the green corn steaming and sizzling in the hot sun, and the oats ripening. A field of clover, the wild roses in the unmown ditches, and the new-mown hay diffused their fresh, sweet fragrances into the air.

After school started, I rode Merrylegs only a few Saturday afternoons, through the hazy, cobwebby days of Indian Summer, during "October's bright blue weather," and not at all in the cold, short days of winter.

My younger brothers, Dale and Dean, loved and rode Merrylegs in their turn, and to their own satisfaction, enjoying her as we older ones had. Neither could remember a time when she wasn't a part of the family.

I went to college and seldom thought of my old friend until the subject came up much, much later. Dean told me what had happened. When he was about seven, and Merrylegs was in the autumn of her life, loyal and faithful as ever, she slipped on the ice and broke her leg. Gene Ward, a hunchbacked man who worked periodically for three generations of our family, undertook the cheerless task that had to be done. With gun in hand, sad eyes, and a downcast face (for he was a kind man), he sent a grief-stricken Dean to the house. The story could end in only one way, but Dean did not have to witness it. Gene did the humane thing and shot our pony. Pa called the rendering works, and they took her away.

Dean told me recently, with a grimace of remembrance, "I didn't like that day." In our family we were expected to be stoic, and grieving was a private matter.

Harry must have felt the loss as keenly as anyone, but he was a man now, with plans for his future, and could relegate this loss to the realm of nostalgia. Through the years, Harry has maintained his love for horses.

BACK EAST

In the early summer of 1930, my parents discussed the possibility of going to Papa's home territory, Fulton County, Pennsylvania. Mama wrote to Aunt Bertha and found that it would be a convenient time for the relatives we were to visit.

Pa had said to her, "Ask her if she will teach you to make potpie while we're there." Potpie was a dish Pa had hungered for ever since he had come to Iowa. That and huckleberry pie were the two foods he had missed the most.

When they had finally decided we could go, Papa said, "I don't think our old 'buggy' could make it up Ligonier Mountain. We'll have to get a new car."

Mama got that funny little quirk at the corner of her mouth that meant something amused her, and she answered, "Yes, indeed. We certainly want to arrive in your hometown looking prosperous."

One evening early in July we went to town to look at the new cars. After we had seen them, Mama, Dean, and I went

*Paul, Dean, and Uncle Burton
in front of the 1930 Dodge.*

to the car while the men of the family dickered with the Dodge dealer. As we sat waiting, we could hear a man yelling in pain. "What's the matter with that man?" I asked Mama.

"The noise is coming from Dr. Wilson's office. The man must be getting a tooth pulled. He ought to be able to stand the pain better than that."

When she said that, I was proud I hadn't made a fuss when I'd recently had two teeth filled, even though it had hurt.

The men came back, and Pa said, "We've bought a car."

Papa drove the new blue sedan home just a week before we left. It had windows to roll up and down—no more scurrying, if it rained, to snap on the curtains with their cracked isinglass windows; those small windows had a few holes in them where I'd nipped out bites of isinglass when no one was looking, because I liked to chew on it. Our new car seemed so luxurious, with its cloth seats and ashtrays in the side walls by the back seat. A small pocket hung on the back of the front seat. I tried to think what we could put in it.

"Well, Skeeter, does it suit you?" Papa asked me.

I nodded my head.

We were up with the chickens on the day we left home. Light streaks were showing in the east. The sounds of the cows mooing and the birds chirping carried clearly through the cool morning air. I was seldom up early enough to enjoy this part of the day.

A fragment of fog hung over the slough by the county line road as we started, five minutes before our planned departure time. Pa tapped the horn gently as we drove by the Ramkers' farmhouse. He seemed to feel as excited as I did.

A cloud of dust followed us on the dirt road, but we smugly rolled up the windows to keep it out. I inhaled the new car smell of the closed car—the mingling of new upholstery, rubber floor mats, and I didn't know what else.

Two-year-old Dean settled down to finish his sleep in the canvas car bed Papa had hung over our feet in the back seat. Dale leaned groggily against Mama in the front seat. Harry and I were too excited to settle down. We each tried to be the first to read the Burma Shave signs spaced along the roads, a few words per sign.

No Lady Likes
To Dance or Dine
Accompanied by
A Porcupine—*Burma Shave*

Around the Curve
Lickety-Split
It's a Beautiful Car
Wasn't It?—*Burma Shave*

"Oh, boy," Harry gloated, "We'll know more Burma Shave signs than anyone else by the time we get home."

We had to drive slowly until the car was broken in, with five hundred miles on the speedometer, but Papa drove steadily. By noon we crossed the River, and Harry and I spelled it out "M-iss-iss-ippi," again and again, until Pa said, "That's enough of that noise."

I looked carefully, but I couldn't see that Illinois looked any different from Iowa.

By the time we reached Rockford, Illinois, around five o'clock, we were tired. Our parents began to look for signs saying, "Tourist Home" or "Rooms for Rent" in the front yards. They chose one, and Papa went in to look it over.

"It looks fine to me," he reported. "She'll serve us supper and breakfast if we like."

It felt good to run up and down the street to stretch our legs while the suitcases were being carried in. We'd had a long day.

After we ate, I got into my nightie and enjoyed the luxury of washing up and going to the toilet in a real bathroom. Then suddenly, surprisingly, I felt uneasy, almost panicky. Something seemed to be pressing down on me. I got into bed and curled into a little ball like a baby, to get away from it. I wanted to be home, where I belonged. Maybe if I told Mama I was sick, we would go home and be safe. What should I do? My mind whirled, but I had to think. If we went home, I wouldn't travel through all those states on the way to Pennsylvania, meet my fifteen cousins there, see the mountains. I decided. No matter how sick I felt in the morning, I would endure it. I wanted to stride into the adventures ahead: to ride up Mount Ligonier, so steep that Pa said it took a strong team of horses to pull a load to the top; to taste huckleberry pie. I wanted to see for myself if dandelions grew in Pennsylvania.

The next day we traveled across the whole state of Indiana, on the great new Highway 30, the "Lincoln Highway." Pa said this same highway went through McConnellsburg, our destination. The road paralleled the railroad tracks much of the way across Indiana. We children stuck our heads out of the windows and waved to the engineers as trains passed up, delighted when they waved back. At last our car was broken in, and we could fly along at forty miles per hour. We couldn't go too fast to suit me, past telephone poles slipping quickly by, past fields of ripening corn, through little towns where people continued their humdrum lives while we were on a great adventure.

By this time Harry and I realized that the Burma Shave signs just kept repeating and we had seen them all. We began to see signs painted on barns, usually "Chew Mail Pouch Tobacco" or "Ceresota Flour." I thought the signs spoiled the barns, but Mama said the farmer could get his barn painted free if he agreed to have the signs on one side.

That night we stayed in one of a huddle of tourist cabins beside the road, a whole little house to ourselves. The water here smelled like rotten eggs because of the minerals in it. We couldn't drink it at all, and I certainly wasn't going to brush my teeth in it. I thought that even if I lived there, I could never get used to it. We were a thirsty family when we went on in the morning.

The third night we stayed with some of Papa's relatives in Ohio. They had several children, who played so politely with us that I thought their parents must have told them to be nice to us. In the yard was a pear tree. The only pears I had ever seen came in a box from the grocer, so I looked with interest at the tree. The young boy in the family noticed and asked if I would like a pear. I said, "Yes, if it's a nice one." That wasn't what I meant to say at all, and I felt embarrassed. What I meant was more like, "Do you mean I could really have such a treat and not have to buy it?" but I didn't know how to say it.

After carefully looking over the fruit, the boy brought me a pear, saying, "Is this one nice enough?"

I said it was, thanked him, and savored the fruit, glad that he didn't seem offended by my rudeness.

The next morning we drove through Weirton, in the north-pointing finger of West Virginia that is squeezed between Ohio and Pennsylvania. I was pleased to add this to the list of states I had visited. The streets were very steep; people and vehicles toiled up them. This industrial town had a smoky, grimy look. I thought life in Iowa, with level land

and clear air to breathe, was much nicer.

In a short time we came to Pittsburgh, the biggest city we had seen. Pa said, "Only a hundred more miles to go."

The weather had been hot, and there were dirty clothes, apple cores and other garbage under Dean's canvas bed, as well as our not-too-clean selves in the car. The new car smell was replaced by the "trip smell," and unpleasant as it was, I sniffed it up as a valued part of our whole unique experience.

"The Juniata River!" Papa announced, seeing a stream flowing beside us.

"We're going up Ligonier Mountain," he said soon, a look of eagerness on his face. He had never gone up this mountain in a car. We ground up the steep grade, changing to the lower gears, but even that was not enough. The motor got so hot that we had to pull over and stop in a wider place in the road. The side of the mountain was all rock, with little seeps of water running down here and there and strings of ferns hanging near the drips of water. Strange little growths clung to the rocks—mosses and lichens in greens and almost yellow tones. Small birds and insects with translucent wings hopped about, making their small noises and eating even smaller wildlife. The layers of the rocks were shades of browns and grays, and in places they were scaling off and falling to the roadside. We couldn't see above the trees to the sky, or the road more than a few rods either way.

We made it to the top, and Pa said, "I guess we had enough horses under the hood even for Ligonier." The rest of the way was easier, and before noon we were looking down at a small town in the valley.

"There she is! McConnellsburg!" It was a good thing the car was broken in, because it was called upon to make good time for the rest of the way.

We drove up with a flourish in front of an interesting looking old stone house, and Papa was out of the car almost before it had stopped. Doors opened, and relatives poured out of the house.

That was the beginning. Papa's four brothers and three sisters and their families welcomed us with big and ever bigger meals, including potpie and huckleberry pie. They took us to visit relatives, to see the battlefield at Gettysburg, and sent us young cousins to movies, until my mind was awhirl. It was a family reunion every day, surprising and confusing and wonderful.

On our way home, sated with reading signs, I lay back and watched the clouds. Cotton candy clouds with feathered edges amused me by changing shapes as they floated gently through the bluest of skies.

Again we drove through the drab and smoke-darkened city of Pittsburgh. Mama told me that the Monongahela and the Allegheny rivers joined here to form the Ohio River. I rolled those names around on my tongue until I knew them for sure.

I thought of all the places we'd been and the people we'd seen. Seeing the relatives was the best part, especially meeting fifteen cousins of my own. I was glad I'd been to Gettysburg, had ridden up and down the mountains, had seen dandelions in Pennsylvania. From now on when Papa talked about Mc-Connellsburg in Fulton County, I would know how it nestled between Sidling Hill and the Tuscaroras.

As we rode along, I noticed Papa's hands on the steering wheel. The scabs he always had from working on the farm were only pink scars. They had healed in the three weeks we'd been gone.

I hoped that Miss Miller would assign us to write a paper for English, "What I did this summer." This year I would have something to write.

3

As Life Appeared to Me

THE BARBERSHOP

A twirling red and white striped pole, standing tall in its vertical frame, identified Van Eman's with barbershops throughout the centuries. It seemed special, almost magical to me, to watch those spiraling stripes disappear endlessly into the top of the pole. I watched, mesmerized, whenever we stopped for popcorn or an ice cream cone at the little stand between the barbershop and the bank.

Gentlewomen were apt to walk by this reputedly sinful place with eyes averted. Mama, in her straightforward way, paid it no attention as we strode by. I wondered what it was about this interesting shop that wasn't quite respectable. The tantalizing glimpse I could get through the big plate glass window did not assuage my curiosity.

Papa took me into this fascinating shop one day, to wait while he got a haircut. There was so much for me to see, sitting on one of the chairs lined up against the wall for the use of men awaiting their turns. Other men—a farmer just coming from the bank, the local realtor, men idling between jobs—came in to read the paper, lounging around and joshing each other in an easy manner, aiming streams of tobacco juice with imperfect accuracy at the ubiquitous spittoons.

Bob, the gregarious proprietor, greeted each arrival by name and was pleased to share the latest news, market reports, and bits of local information that previous visitors had imparted to him. His assistant, Wayne, was more quiet but, when addressed, held up his end of the commentary with a smile. The atmosphere was that of an informal though sometimes uncouth men's club, with no membership requirements.

In the back was a pool hall, rumored to be the location of the iniquities, if indeed any existed. I was not daring enough to leave my chair and go to the double doors, but I looked and looked through them for the evil. I was never lucky enough to recognize any. I could see men in vests, their shirt-sleeves bloused above elastic armbands, walking around carrying long poles. A man would bend over a big green-covered table, sight down his pole, and with a quick jerk, click it against some balls. The balls would roll around, hitting each other and the sides of the big table, and some might go in the pockets at the corners of the table. Boisterous laughter indicated that the men were having a good time. From somewhere I had absorbed the idea that gambling was connected with this game, and that money was lost that might better have been spent on food and clothing for needy children or dropped in the collection plate on Sunday. Certainly none of my family or their friends associated with this disreputable sport.

Along the right side of the wall dividing the two rooms was a cubicle, with a sign saying, "Baths — 25 cents!" Why, I wondered, would anyone want to pay to take a bath in a barbershop? Later, at home, Mama explained that some laborers lived in rooms without facilities to get clean all over. Travelers, some of them homeless (I knew she meant tramps), were glad to pay for the use of a tub, hot water, soap, and a towel.

A most unique feature of the shop, inside the large plate glass window facing south, was a pair of fruit trees growing in tubs. Each produced a few huge fruits — oranges or lemons — every winter, seeming a miracle in the cold Iowa weather. The sun and the steam, plus the heat from the stove back by the pool hall wall, must have fooled the dwarfed trees into thinking they were in a subtropical climate.

Those awaiting their turns for haircuts faced three barber chairs. Back of those chairs was an expanse of plate glass mirrors on the wall, with cabinets below. These contained shelves of lotions in their colorful bottles, and rows of elaborately decorated shaving mugs.

"Well, Paul," said Bob when it was Papa's turn, "is that new farmer at your house husking corn yet?"

He was referring to my baby brother, born just before my fifth birthday in July.

"No," Papa replied with a grin, "but he does all right with the milking." After he got into the chair, the barber cranked it up to a convenient height with a foot pedal. He draped a cloth with little vertical blue figures over Pa's shoulders and snugged it around his neck. I couldn't figure out how it fastened. As the barber worked, the chair was rotated. He combed Pa's hair up the sides of his head with a narrow, tapered comb, and with his sharp shears snip-snipped, very quickly, close to the comb. Using the comb to hold up the hair, he measured between his fingers to cut the top to the correct length. Clippers trimmed the hair at the back of the neck. The barber whisked a soft brush with talcum powder shaken into it over Papa's neck and face to remove loose hair. Then Papa decided what good-smelling lotion he preferred, and the barber rubbed it into his hair. Pa's hair got a straight part and a final meticulous combing. His appearance left no doubt that he had a new haircut. The protective cloth was swished off, and Bob cheerfully called out, "Who's next?" while brushing a whisk broom over Papa's clothes as he climbed out of the chair.

While Papa had been waiting, the local banker came in for his regular morning shave and sat down in Wayne's chair. For this procedure the back of the chair was lowered and he reclined there comfortably. A small towel was wet in the pedestal sink in front of the chair. The water was so hot that the barber had to slap the towel against the sides of the sink several times to help wring out the water before applying the steaming towel to the waiting face. Wayne stropped the straight-edged razor on a leather strap hanging from a cabinet along the mirrored wall. I watched with fascination as he slid that dangerous blade—"snap"—up one side and—"snap"—down the other without even looking.

Taking down the patron's personal shaving mug from its place on the shelf, the barber wet its brush and worked up a lather on the little, round, flat bar of mild soap in the bottom of the mug. The still warm towel came off, and the foam was applied carefully to the readied face, leaving gaps for nose and mouth and avoiding the eye area. Wayne held the skin taut between two fingers of his left hand and carefully scraped the blade against the whiskers, section by section. A quick rinse removed any remaining islands of suds. The newly shaved man chose bay rum to be rubbed in as an emollient. Papa shaved every day, but he never achieved the glow and bare-bottom look of a barber's shave.

This pampered customer then continued his ritual by climbing up into one of the two shoe-shining chairs by the door. He lit up a cigar, adding its pungent smoke to the barbershop aroma, while he exchanged small talk with the elderly shoe-shine "boy."

When I was very young, Mama took me to the barbershop across the street to get my hair cut. It wasn't nearly as exciting as Bob's shop, but Mama felt more comfortable here. It had no pool hall or hangers-on with their stories, which might not be suitable for a child's ears. When the barber saw how short I was, he put a board over the arms of the chair to raise me to the right height. I enjoyed sitting like a queen on her throne, wriggling my arms under the enveloping cloak. Then I looked at the reflections in the big mirror and speculated about the scents and colors of the tempting lotions reflected there. I was always disappointed that a little girl got no lotion on her newly cut hair, no matter how carefully I had decided which would be the best choice of all. Even my two little brothers got lotion after their haircuts. It was outrageous.

When I was fourteen, I went for the first time to a beauty salon for a permanent. Here the beautician treated my hair with lotions and creams and pampered me with special attention and conversation. My perceived injustice to the plumage of the fair sex was rectified at last.

THE WALK HOME

Miss Eveland rings the bell and school is out. We laugh and chatter as we gather our tin dinner-pails and wraps that are too warm for this October day. We rush into the hazy air and skip and walk together to the crossroads. The others turn toward their homes, and Harry and I go on. Deep in my thoughts, I lag behind as Harry hurries on ahead.

An early frost has lightly touched the growing things, but today the sun is warm. Black-eyed Susans nod their golden heads to greet me. The scarlet sumac flaunts its blazing colors as I near the twin rows of trees. This lane of trees is familiar but somehow mysterious. Some places are in shadow, but in others sun dapples the dirt road through the trembling leaves. Insects hum, and the leaves, beginning to turn to their fall colors, rustle and sigh in the cooling breeze.

A farmer, glimpsed through the trees, turns the soil in the fall plowing. The harness creaks, and the horses snort and mouth their bits as they turn to start the new row. "Easy, now, easy," guides the farmer. Reins slap the backs of the team, adding to the symphony of sounds. Birds chirp as they follow the furrow and feed on bugs and worms behind the plow.

I walk on, feeling a sadness for the summer's end, but attuned to the beauty of now—almost in a dream. A sound I can't explain thuds my heart and speeds my lagging feet beyond the woods. A rabbit hops out ahead of me and disappears into the matted grass.

Horses graze in our pasture on my right. The grass is sparse and dry, but this land has never known a plow, and spring will renew its lush growth. The small slough, where the pussy willows sprout in spring, is dry and cracked in fall. Milkweeds burst their pods, sending gossamer seeds to float and fall and catch in clumps along the road.

Then there is our orchard, with its winey smell of fruit forgotten in the grass. The hens announce their day's work done: "Cut-cut-cut cadakit—I laid an egg in the basket." Jack lopes out to meet me, his plume of tail wagging, seeming to smile as his tongue lolls out. I jump up and down in our usual greeting, and he accepts my invitation to leap up for a hug. We feint back and forth a time or two, and I scratch his head through the long fur as we go toward the house.

And here is home, and mother, and spicy cookies cooling on the kitchen table.

YOU DON'T BELONG

One June evening Mama sat perusing our local paper, *The Recorder.* "I see there's going to be a celebration in town on Friday. They're going to have rides brought in, and exhibits showing all kinds of new things."

"Something else to separate us from our money, no doubt," Papa joked.

On the day of the celebration, Papa mentioned it at breakfast: "Do you want to go to the doings in town, Dorothy?"

"Oh, yes, let's do," Mama answered quickly. "The kids will enjoy the rides, and I'd like to see the exhibits. Helen says they're going, and Ellen. Others, too."

"I have hay down, but maybe it can wait. I'll come in early for dinner, and we'll see how the weather looks then."

When dinner time came, the urgency of haying was pushed back as the cloudless day promised good weather.

Papa said we could go to town. We joined the throngs of people walking up and down the blocked-off main street, looking at exhibits and greeting friends.

The lilting music of the merry-go-round, its twinkling lights and horses in colors that never were, beckoned. Mama gave me a nickel to buy a ticket, and I hurried to climb on a gilt-trimmed blue horse with eager painted eyes and flaring nostrils. The frightening lurch as we started made me grab the shiny pole to which my horse was attached. After a few turns I could survey the crowds and wave to Dale in his baby buggy. I clucked my tongue and slapped the leather reins as if to urge on my horse to even greater speed. When the ride ended, I laughed because my legs didn't work right for a few steps.

Next we went into the big tent set up in the street between Buchholz's and Pooley's. On the sawdust-covered floor of the tent were groups of tables, forming booths for advertising and for selling things. I soon grew tired of looking in the murky light at roofing samples, bake sales, and needlework items being sold by the Ladies' Aid. Mama, who was talking to Genie Downs, said I could wander around by myself. It was safe enough, and I was so keyed up with excitement that I didn't feel the need to cling to an adult. I saw a group of girls, who seemed to be about my age, standing behind some tables in the corner. It looked like fun to stand there so importantly, chattering with each other and handing out papers to passersby. Still in my buoyant state, I walked behind the table and stood, too. At once two girls came over to me and scolded, "You can't stand here! You don't belong!"

Crestfallen, deflated, I walked away, deciding never to be so bold again. I couldn't help wondering why these girls, who seemed so much like me, belonged and I didn't. My fun was spoiled, and I stayed close to Mama for the rest of that colorless afternoon.

Several years later a promoter came to Greene and directed a big performance of variety acts by local people. By that time I knew several town girls from Sunday School. A group of them were chosen to do the "Highland Fling." No doubt they were chosen from town school classrooms, whereas I wasn't chosen because I went to country school. At various times the girls showed me the steps they were learning, hopping on one foot with the other foot bent at the knee, gracefully moving in different positions. It did look like such fun. I wondered if I could have learned to do the dance if I had been chosen. I thought I could have, but a lingering doubt remained that maybe I wasn't good enough to be chosen.

I often heard girls I knew at Sunday School talking about going to meetings of a church group they belonged to. I think they were "Mother's Jewels" and, when they were older, "King's Daughters." Occasionally someone would ask me if I were going to the meeting, as if it were a very ordinary question. I was embarrassed at not even knowing what they were talking about.

Eventually I was asked to attend. At the meeting I knew all the girls at least slightly, but they seemed like strangers as they played out their roles—taking part in the business meeting, discussing the religious lesson, handing around refreshments—in this setting so new to me. They all knew what was expected of them, while I sat ill at ease, worrying that I might do the wrong thing or not do the right thing.

Because I wasn't asked again, I assumed I hadn't "made the grade," that I didn't belong. I wanted to be a part of the group but wouldn't risk embarrassment by asking about it. Maybe Mama sensed my ambivalent feelings and thought my hesitancy meant I didn't want to go. As an adult, I understand that girls my age were not only welcome to go but really were needed to perform the little missionary efforts of the group.

One summer every town girl (or so it seemed to me) wore strap sandals with buckles that slid over and hid the button fastener. The shoe clerk had shown them to me, saying, "These are the shoes all the girls are wearing this summer."

I tried them on, but my toes bumped against the ends of the shoes and hurt. As always when I bought shoes, the clerk said, "Oh, these are big enough. See how much room there is?"

The trouble was, they were too wide and too short, and I'd suffered through this poor fit too often before. He showed me some sandals with ribbon bows like a dancer's shoes. They felt much better, and I thought they were prettier. They were my choice.

The first time I wore them to Sunday School, I discovered that the clerk had been right. All the other girls were wearing the button style. They were a group belonging together, and once more I was the one who didn't fit in. I imagined that they looked at me with disdain, though not one girl ever mentioned that my feet weren't in step with the style that summer.

COUNTRY SCHOOL

Pleasant Grove #8 was the name of the rural school I attended for seven years. Harry started a year before I did, and immediately I thought it sounded interesting.

Mama sat rocking me by the window in the small north bedroom as he came sauntering home one day, banging his dinnerpail against his knee. She called out to him, and he ran over to us.

"What did you learn in school today?" she asked.

"I learned a song about a pony," he answered, and he sang it to us.

Mama looked proud of her big boy, and I was impressed.

The next fall I was old enough to start school. Mama got me a dinnerpail, a new tin cup, two penny pencils, a box of Crayolas, and a Red Chief tablet. She packed a lunch for each of us, gave me the primer Harry had used, and sent me to school with my big brother.

When I got there, I hung back shyly until the big girls showed me around. They told me where to put my dinnerpail and hang my cup, which toilet was for the girls, and how to play their games. Ring-Around the Rosy was fun, and Prisoner's Base. We played Pussy Wants a Corner inside the schoolhouse at recess when the weather was bad outside.

I liked the Victrola best. It had a big, fluted horn just like the ones pictured later in a Victrola ad with a dog sitting in front of the horn and the caption "His Master's Voice." The records were thick, ridged cylinders about five inches long, and they slipped over a rod on the top of the player. I had never seen a machine this old or had a chance to play records, to hear the quick, shrill sounds emerging from the speaker with a somewhat hollow sound, as though from a distance. The school had few records, but I was content to hear them again and again. My favorites were "Listen to the Mocking Bird," "School Days, School Days, Good Old Golden Rule Days," and especially the soothing melody and dreamy rhythm of "Swing Low, Sweet Chariot." The girls teased me gently about wanting to hear it so many times.

Mrs. Howe, our teacher, rang her big brass handbell, and the pupils scurried to their seats. She took me to the smallest desk, right in front of Harry, and said that it would be mine. When we stood up to say the "Pledge of Allegiance," I moved my lips, but I didn't know the words. That night I had Harry repeat the pledge to me until I had learned it, so I wouldn't be embarrassed the next day.

My desk was a single one, but some were double, for two pupils to sit side by side. With only seven pupils enrolled the year I started to school, no one had to use those. I thought it would be fun to sit with a friend in such an arrangement. Each seat back was the front of the desk behind it. The inkwell at the top right corner didn't have any ink in it, so I put

Pleasant Grove #8.

my pencil there. It fell right out, so I laid it in the little trough along the desk top, took my tablet and made marks in it, pretending to write the ABCs.

When the teacher had time, she brought me a picture to color. I tried to stay in the lines, but I'd never had a real picture to color before, only shapes like apples and bananas that Mama drew for me. I cut out the picture with Harry's scissors, and the teacher gave me a glob of paste on a piece of paper. When I finished pounding the picture into my tablet, the paste was gone. The first time I licked my fingers, I learned the childhood pleasure of eating library paste.

We pupils started in primary, corresponding to kindergarten. Harry was in first grade. I was eager to unlock the secrets of my primer. The first page read:

> Mama, see kitty.
> See kitty.
> See mama.
> See kitty, mama.

The teacher used phonics cards with the letter and a picture on the front for the pupil to see. On the back was a story the teacher read aloud as she held up the card. The letter "K" pictured a kitten. The story told about a kitten who got a fish bone caught in her throat, and she coughed with a kitteny sound, "k-k-k."

We had only one reader each year. In second grade I finished mine early in the spring. The teacher asked Mama to buy me another one. The first story in the new book was about a little boy playing outside at dusk. The stars seemed so near to him that he got a stick and tried to knock one down. The second story was called "Leerie, the Lamplighter," about a child who watched out his window every evening when a man came with his ladder and torch to light the gas street lamps. I have never forgotten the joy, the excitement, and the power I felt when I realized that the world of adventure on the printed page was now mine. I am grateful to the teacher and to my mother for providing this book, which opened the world of reading for me.

My only problem with reading after that was in finding enough to read. The shelf of books at school consisted of someone's cast-offs, not books for children. I read them anyway. One was called *The Iron Trail,* telling of the building of the railroad across the United States. I sounded out the words and tried to figure out their meaning from the context.

When I was six, a woodshed was built just south of the schoolhouse. The carpenter talked and joked with us pupils. One noon hour while he was on the roof pounding nails into the shingles, the kids asked him to spell various words, trying to stump him. At last I got up my nerve and asked him to spell "banana." He answered promptly, "Ba-na-na."

"Aw, that isn't right," I answered, thinking that no word would have an "a" for every other letter. I had been half expecting him to tease me with a wrong answer, knowing I wouldn't be sure if he did. He solemnly insisted that he was right. It was some time before I could read the word myself and know that he had not been teasing. After the shed was built, we had a good place to play a game I called "Anny Anny Over," trying to throw a ball over the roof. My swinging arm was barely equal to the task.

In my first year of school, Mrs. Howe acquainted us pupils with the story of the *Constitution*, a famous sailing ship. It was commissioned in 1790 by George Washington. During a big battle in the War of 1812, a cannonball from an enemy ship bounced off the oak sides of the ship. Because of this the sailors nicknamed her "Old Ironsides."

In the early part of the 1900s, the ship was a rotting hulk in Boston Harbor. A campaign was started to save her. Schoolchildren were asked to give their pennies to help with the restoration. We were excited to be a part of a project so linked with history. Mama gave Harry and me each five Lincoln pennies as our donation.

Through the years, this story receded from my memory. But in 1968 my husband and I, with our five children, visited Boston Harbor and went aboard the *Constitution*, the oldest commissioned ship in the U.S. Navy. Gradually I recalled with a thrill my part in saving "Old Ironsides."

When it began to get cool in the fall, field mice occasionally crept into the cloakroom entrance to our school. On one such occasion I watched as the nose of a curious mouse discovered the greater warmth of the classroom. When a gray body followed the nose under the door, I gave the alarm.

"Mouse, mouse!" I called out, pointing to the door where the mouse stood trembling. Instinctively the startled teacher jumped up on her chair. She soon took up the chase, wielding the broom. Some of the pupils ran for weapons. Harry grabbed the coal shovel; Ruth took the poker. The rest of us jumped frenziedly up and down, adding our shrieks to the din. Dust and chalk dust flew as we beat the floor vigorously. Because the intention for the mouse was murder, not escape, Ivan and I bravely guarded the two front doors. The poor mouse ended up a bloody gray form, to be picked up by the tail and thrown outdoors. All that was left was a hint of dead mouse smell and dust particles gleaming and settling in the sun's rays shining through the windows.

The walk to school was often pleasant. On winter days the new snow lay sparkling in the sun, heaped up in swirling mounds like whipped cream at the sides of the roads. It crunched under our overshoes as we walked. When the weather was really cold, Papa would hitch a team to the sled and give us a ride to school.

One cold day when we walked, I could see three suns in the sky. We stumbled half frozen into the barely warm schoolroom and told the others what we had seen. Ruth, who always knew everything, said with assurance, "Sun dogs. Those are sun dogs." I was vexed, wanting her to be wrong, because she knew more than I did. As usual, she was right.

On such days, in spite of long underwear, long lisle stockings bunched over it, leggings buttoned from ankle to knee, four-buckle galoshes, warm wool mittens that Aunt Jen had knit, a heavy coat, and a stocking cap, I arrived at school chilled. The teacher, who came early to start the fire, always looked us over for white, frostbitten spots and helped rub some warmth into our numb hands and feet. Once—only once—I put my tongue on the metal door latch to taste the frost, and found myself a prisoner, my tongue fastened to the door. To get free, I had to leave a portion of skin on the frozen door.

In the spring we walked by our orchard, filled with fragrant apple blossoms, and pussy willows growing in the ditch beyond. Quails whistled "bob-bob-white" from the fields, and killdeer flying overhead named themselves emphatically with shrill cries. The sight of tender green leaves in the line of trees was welcome after the brown of winter. Sweet Williams grew in profusion in the ditches north of the trees, followed in turn by Johnny Jump-ups, tiny sweet wild strawberries covered with seeds, and our state flower, the wild rose.

When they could work without mittens in the nippy April weather, the big boys used their pocketknives to whittle off a flexible willow wand to test it for whistle-making. There were only a few days when the wood was just right, when the buds swelled but the leaves hadn't erupted. The twig had to be green and slippery with sap under the bark. I watched the process many times, until at last in second grade I made a whistle that worked.

It looked easy. I borrowed Harry's knife and cut off a five-inch piece about as big around as my thumb, using Ruth's whistle as a pattern. She had cut through the circumference of the bark about an inch and a half from one end. A slit went straight down through one half of this line, perhaps an eighth-inch into the wood. A wedge started half an inch from this cut and went diagonally toward the bottom of the slit. This tiny piece of wood and bark was removed.

Next came the trickiest part, where I had ruined many an embryo whistle. The bark had to be loosened by twisting and rubbing gently until the cut piece could be slipped off. If the bond between bark and wood was slippery enough, all was well. This step successfully completed, I cut a horizontal slice of bare wood from the wedge to the end of the whistle, carefully slipped the bark back over the end of the wood, and blew. A reedy sound delighted me. I had made a whistle!

We left our whistles with our dinnerpails during school hours.

Ruth's older sister Blanche was ill and out of school for several weeks in March. When she came back, we learned that she had sugar diabetes (its official name at that time). Insulin recently had become available to treat this disease, which previously had been fatal. Blanche needed insulin shots several times a day, and she gave them to herself at school. We girls watched. She took a syringe and pushed its needle into a small bottle of insulin, withdrew the required dose, then sponged her thigh with alcohol and drove the needle into the flesh. It was almost inconceivable to us that she could have the self-discipline to do it, but she had been taught well and knew that she would die without it. The little bottles had rubber tops just the right size to be pencil erasers, so she gave them to us when we asked for them. They didn't erase very well, but we felt connected to the strangeness of the whole illness and its treatment.

Blanche was on a special diet and had to eat a bite of lunch at recess, usually a piece of fruit. She often brought a big chunk of red salmon, with a big chunk of butter on it, for her lunch at noon. My mouth watered when I saw it, but she said it got tiresome. She couldn't have candy or other sweets, but she didn't complain about these restrictions at school, as I thought I might have. Once in awhile she got a "reaction," from too much insulin. Then she had to eat something with sugar in it.

Miss Shook was our flapper teacher of the twenties. She wore her skirts short, and when she bent over a desk to help a child, we could see her panties, pretty in pastel colors. We laughed about it at recess, but we were careful that she didn't hear us joke, because we liked her.

Most of the time I was the only member of my class, so I could learn at my own speed and get help from the teacher when I needed it. When I was learning the multiplication tables, Miss Shook gave me the table, and I learned it by writing it on the boards painted black on each side of the real blackboard. When I was to learn the 11's, however, she just told me 11 times 1 and 11 times 2, then said to write the rest. I was quite upset and fumed inwardly that she had not given me the whole table. At last I wrote down 33, 44, 55, and asked her if that was right. She just smiled and said, "Of course." No one had told me that in multiplication you could add the number to the last sum and get the next number, and strangely enough, I still didn't realize it after this lesson. Arithmetic was never my favorite subject.

Our school had a reed organ, trimmed with carving, with little round shelves for lamps above the keyboard on either side. Most of our teachers were able to play simple songs, pumping the foot pedals vigorously to fill the bellows with air, which then was forced through the reeds to produce the sounds.

Once a week, more often in winter when we were tethered inside the building by bad weather, we gathered around as the teacher played the organ, reading the words from the same book she used. We sang songs such as "The Old Oaken Bucket," "My Bonnie Lies Over the Ocean," and "Comin' Through the Rye." We sang lustily, if not musically. I found no fault with this until after I transferred to town school and realized that my musical education had been slighted.

Penmanship, taught through the Palmer method, was the cause of great despair for me. No matter how I tried to make the "push and pulls" stand smooth as a fence across my paper, they were uneven. My ovals, which were supposed to look like beautiful interlocking circles of smoke flowing back from a train, seemed instead to be blown by the wind into weird and uneven shapes. The teacher got a little exasperated with me. Why, she wondered, couldn't I do this simple thing right when I did others things quite well? I tried and tried, but my muscles seemed always to jerk out of control and ruin the page. In frustration, I chewed the end of my wooden penholder to slivers, and tears mixed with the drops of ink that fell from the pen point. I am thankful that, in my mature years, a word processor has rescued me from the curse of illegible handwriting.

When we studied geography, and sometimes during history class, we went to the back of the room, where maps hung high on the wall. With the little hook on the end of her narrow, wooden pointer, our teacher would unlock the case of rolled-up maps, catch the correct map with the same hook, and roll it down. I was always enthralled as she pointed out what we were studying, wanting to look longer, and to dream what going to those faraway places would be like. Maps didn't have to be changed often, but our teacher did have to explain to us that the map of Europe had changed after the World War, and that we should really have a new one.

When I finished my work early, the teacher might say to me, "Margaret, you may use the 'Latta Book.'" This was a catalog-sized book with soft covers, from the Latta Company, which sold all kinds of school supplies. In the front were pictures to trace and color, and in the back were stories. When I was in fourth grade, I traced a picture called "One Misty, Moisty Morning," a rainy scene in which a little girl carrying an umbrella walked in the rain. I colored it softly, not pressing down hard with my crayons. The blues, greens, and a little black, so soft it looked gray, made it look blurry, like a scene one might see out of a window on a rainy day. The teacher said it was well done, but my real reward was that I pleased myself by coloring in a way so suited to the name of the picture. I kept it a long time.

In the back of the Latta Book was a story about an eagle that swooped down and picked up a little child in its terrifying talons. It was scary, but we didn't have eagles like that in Iowa, or so I hoped. The story must have had a happy ending or I would remember that part of the story, too.

TOWN SCHOOL

In 1929, when Harry and I were in grades eight and seven, we started going to school in town. I am not sure why our parents decided to have us make this change, but I was in favor of it.

Margaret Ott, twelve years old.

Although he was only thirteen, Harry drove us to school in a Model T pickup. No one needed a driver's license at that time, and he learned from our parents what he needed to know about driving. In rainy weather, when this little car drove through a puddle, muddy water splashed up through gaps in the floorboards. Years passed and cars improved before I could ride through a puddle without automatically lifting my feet.

Nadine, Hazel, and the others my age who had been in my Sunday School class were in Harry's grade, and I had a whole new set of friends in my class. The town students had been in first grade while we country students had taken a year in primary.

The best part of going to town school was the joy of having so many pupils in my class. I liked the feeling of belonging and made friends quickly. Dorothy lived in the country and brought her lunch as I did. We immediately became good friends. Dorothy's cousin Lucille, with whom I had often played, was in my class also. The girls' mothers were sisters, and their pictures, as well as that of their brother, Percy, were in Mama's Sunday School "Plus Ultra" picture. Mama said they had been good friends when they were children and their mothers had been friends, too. It made our friendship special, almost as if we were relatives. Dorothy and Lucille had many cousins around Greene. I envied them, as I had no cousins nearby. We decided I could call myself their cousin, and I felt as if I truly were.

Later that year Mr. Don Walter came to our school to start a band. One day the fifth and sixth graders came into our assembly room, and Mr. Walter demonstrated several band instruments for us. He arranged to meet with those who were interested in starting an instrument. My parents told me they could not afford to buy an instrument for me. They may have been influenced by my poor record as a piano player.

When Dorothy and several other friends filed out for practice the last period of the day, I longed to go along, to belong to that privileged group. Finally, the next year, my parents bought a cornet for me. Although I was always embarrassed by the cheap cardboard-like case the cornet came in, band was the highlight of the rest of my school years. Dorothy also played a cornet.

Our band uniforms consisted of a green cape, overseas-style cap, and white wash slacks with a green silk stripe down the sides of the legs. These stripes had to be taken off and sewed on again every time the pants were washed. Mama showed me how to take a small stitch on the right side and a long stitch underneath, and I grew quite expert at it.

When my country life broadened to include associations with town children, I had many cultural adjustments to make. None was harder for me than to decide what to call my father. The children in our family were taught to say "papa," but I soon realized that this was old-fashioned and that others my age said "daddy." By the time I started going to town school, I felt uncomfortable with either name. It was a problem I never really solved. The best I could do was to refer to "my dad" with my friends and to continue with "papa" at home.

Two activities I had not learned in country school were jacks and roller skating. Seventh-grade girls had almost outgrown playing jacks, but Dorothy and the other girls taught me how to bounce the little red rubber ball and pick up the jacks in variations of the game. Once I had learned how, I was satisfied to put my jacks away. Not so with roller skating. I swooped joyously along on the rough sidewalks at last, any noon hour that another girl would skate with me. A rink was opened downtown, and skating around and around its slick surface was a popular activity for young people of all ages. The metal wheels of the skates roared on the wooden floor as we skated, almost drowning out the musical accompaniment. To carry on a conversation, two people had to skate very close together. Many a courtship was furthered privately in this very public place.

Encouraged by our mothers, Dorothy and I had gone back and forth to each other's homes and had taken little trips with each other's families, such as to the County Fair. The first friend I stayed overnight with was Dorothy. The bond between us grew constantly. On school days we ate in only a few minutes the typical peanut butter sandwich-cookies-apple lunches we carried. We were free to do as we pleased for the rest of the hour. One noon when we were in eighth grade, we walked downtown, with no more purpose than to get some exercise and to talk. Following a pattern established during many such walks, we wandered into the variety store and looked at the pretty handkerchiefs. We window-shopped at the cosmetics in the drug store window and the dresses in Buchholtz's expanse of windows.

Walking back toward school, we crossed the railroad tracks and walked past the grain elevator. Noticing a sparking object in the gravelly dirt of the street that turned toward the elevator, I picked it up. The object was a metal ring with a translucent piece of mica inside. We speculated about its possible use and amused ourselves with silly suggestions. Dorothy named it "the Camel's Eye." As we started to go on to school, she said she would keep it.

"No," I objected, "I found it. I should be the one to keep it."

"I gave it a name; it's mine," she responded.

Dorothy Mather,
a Lucas "cousin" and a companion
in the adventure of
"the Camel's Eye."

We glared at each other.

In only a matter of seconds, Dorothy said, "It isn't that important."

"No. We're making a mountain out of a molehill," I answered. "Neither of us should keep it."

"Let's bury it," responded Dorothy.

We scrabbled up a grave in the hard dirt of the street and buried the Camel's Eye, never to be seen by either of us again. We vowed that if ever a dispute arose between us henceforth, one of us had only to say, "Remember the Camel's Eye," and the argument would end at once. We were pleased with our melodramatic conclusion. Our friendship was never again threatened by such a paltry difference.

Dorothy and I remained close friends: in school, in band, in church, and in shared family recreations, even when we attended different colleges. We were attendants at each other's weddings and rejoiced when each other's babies were born. We visited whenever we could, but Dorothy and I never lived in the same town again. Each of us built deep and lasting friendships with other women. None of these friendships, however, had started with our grandmothers, and no other friend ever seemed quite so much a part of me. Dorothy's early death saddens me yet.

Art work was required of us in junior high. When we wrote papers for various subjects, we made construction paper covers for them. I enjoyed reading about a subject in reference books and writing a report. It wasn't as easy for me to make a cover. We had to draw construction paper letters for the title by using a ruler, not by tracing patterns. My classmates had been doing this for years, but I had never made a paper letter in my life. I was in the single-letter stage when others were making fancy double letters with two colors of paper. When I pasted the letters on my first booklet, I nostalgically discovered that town school paste tasted the same as country school paste.

Learning new ways of doing lessons in a class with more than twenty pupils was an interesting challenge. We often corrected each other's papers in class, and I was glad when we passed our papers forward so I would get Ralph's papers. He was Dorothy's brother, and his papers were so well done that they were easy to check.

Also new to me was the practice of going to another room for part of our classes. Our two junior high teachers alternated in using the rooms. After I got used to taking along everything I needed, I found it a nice break in the routine.

In eighth grade I got my first fountain pen, a bright

green Palmer pen. I used this same pen until I was out of college, spoiling many a sheet of paper with the ink that dripped from it.

Also in eighth grade, the Kodak Company gave every girl who was twelve that year a nice little Brownie camera. It was the twelfth anniversary of some event in the life of Kodak. All my classmates got them and went around busily taking pictures. Alas, I was thirteen that year, and nothing could be done about that.

When we moved up to high school in ninth grade, our class size more than doubled because students from the rural schools joined us. I was pleased to become reacquainted with Ivan and Luverna, who had been in my grade in rural school at times in the lower grades.

It was satisfying to me to be an old hand in this school, and to help the new students make the adjustment from country school. At last I felt like one of the "in" group.

Because of various illnesses during my high school years, I was often out of school. When I missed school, I felt as if I slipped into a valley, and just as I climbed out, I was sick again. With the help of conscientious teachers, I made up all the work.

Being in the band gave me the recognition, the feeling of belonging, and the sense of achievement I had wanted all my life. When I put on the green and white uniform, I was one of a group, proud to play in the concerts, go to contests, and march in parades representing Greene High School.

4

Friends and Neighbors

A KINDNESS LONG REMEMBERED

Her name was Mrs. McClennan, and she came through the north lane of trees in the soft spring air to call on Mama. She drove a horse and buggy, as few farm folk had cars in 1921. I remember her as a small, gentle woman with a sweet smile, prim in her dark dress and little hat. She wasn't one of the ladies Mama regularly neighbored with, but we had recently moved to a farm adjoining McClennan land. Having gone on visits like this with Mama, I understood that calling on new neighbors to get acquainted and offering any help that might be needed was considered a proper gesture.

Three-and-a-half that spring, I sat on the floor playing with my doll and listening to the ladies talk of mutual friends, families, and recipes.

As she was leaving, our new neighbor asked if she could borrow my doll for awhile. I thought it strange but didn't question the inexplicable ways of grown-ups. Mama smiled, and I knew it must be all right. It was an early, unnamed doll, here and gone before Bobby, Dorothy, and Richard, the well-remembered and beloved "children" of my childhood.

Some time later the doll was returned to me, but now she was dressed in a new outfit. Quickly I undressed her, and I saw with surprise that she had a wardrobe of handmade clothes, more beautiful than I could ever have imagined. Thrilled and delighted with each little garment, I examined every one carefully as I dressed her completely again. First came the white nainsook panties, with elastic at the waist and a lazy daisy embroidered to show which was the front. Her slip, of the same material, had a tiny button and buttonhole on one shoulder to make it easier to pull over her feet. The pink print dress had lace at the neckline and on the hem. A coat had three buttons down the front and a soft little velvet collar. It was so perfect that I would have been happy to wear it myself if it had been in my size. Most wonderful of all was a tiny hat adorned with a real feather! Ladies wore feathers on their hats then, so my doll was right in style. I asked Mama why the lady had done this for me. She explained that Mrs. McClennan had no little girl of her own, and she liked to make doll clothes.

Once again I undressed and dressed the doll, not yet quite believing the doll's clothes were really mine. Then we set off with baby in her buggy to go from place to place in the house, to visit imaginary friends. When Mama bathed her baby, Robert, I bathed my doll (but I didn't use real water), and I dressed her while Mama dressed Robert. We visited as if we were really two mothers enjoying our babies.

More than sixty years later I remember the joy it gave me to play with that wardrobe of garments, dressing my doll over and over in her new clothes. Even more, I remember the special feeling of being pampered by Mrs. McClennan's unexpected kindness to me.

THE WATKINS MAN

In the 1920s several itinerant salesmen brought their wares into our rural homes on a regular basis. I remember them as being almost without faces or personalities. They were simply the Fuller Brush man, the Watkins man, the Rawleigh man. It made a nice break in the household routine to look at the products so interestingly presented, and it saved running around on hurried trips to town to find their equal in a store.

The Fuller Brush man handed the lady of the house a firm little vegetable brush as he came in. More than one housewife missed those brushes when they were no longer available.

As part of every fastidious woman's grooming routine, she brushed her hair a hundred strokes each evening. No brush could begin to compare with the Fuller hairbrush with its semicircle of natural bristles around the handle. And Fuller's clothes brushes whisked off lint and dirt in no time. The salesman always had his little joke: "The trouble with my job is that my brushes are so good you ladies never need to replace them. I'm going to have to carry a new line." From time to time he did add new items and found his products easy to sell.

My favorite salesman was the Watkins man. He came in confidently, soft spoken and clean shaven. He spread open his case to show off his wares. His flavorings and spices were the best we could buy. We knew because he told us so. We also knew it was true from years of satisfaction with the products. I especially liked the variety of flavorings: black walnut, mint, orange, lemon, strawberry (that one did have an artificial taste, but it was fun to try). Mama always knew what she needed, but she tried a new item now and then to please me. While that unhurried transaction took place, I had plenty of time to look over all the varieties to see what I might ask for.

Often he had a new product to introduce. "Does your family like pudding? I see this pretty young lady does. I have a real time-saver here in a prepared pudding. Mrs. Dailey bought the chocolate today, and my wife swears by the butterscotch." He held open a can for us to sniff. "Doesn't that smell nice and rich? Each can makes twenty servings. Just add your own milk and eggs. Next time I'll have the lemon. Which would you like to try today?"

I waited hopefully for Mama's decision, until she finally said, "I'll try a box of the chocolate, though it does seem a little high."

"It's the savings in time that makes it worthwhile, my

customers tell me," he replied glibly. "How are you fixed for shampoo, Mrs. Ott?"

"We may need some before your next trip. We'd better have a bottle," Mama might answer. "Six heads to wash every week or two uses it up pretty fast."

"It's the 'Mulsified Coconut Oil you use, isn't it? That's the most popular, but we do have others you might try. All of them are excellent."

I had no thought of disagreeing with his assessment of Watkins' shampoo until I went for my first permanent. The operator asked if I had washed my hair. I replied that I had.

"What kind of shampoo did you use?" she asked suspiciously.

"Watkins' 'Mulsified Coconut Oil Shampoo." I boomed out the syllables proudly, expecting her to commend me for my fine choice.

"Oh!" she replied disdainfully. "Come over to the sink, and I'll wash that out. And next time you don't need to wash your hair before you come in."

I felt deflated and gauche. Not only was I too simple to know a shampoo was included with the permanent, but the shampoo I'd thought was so good was substandard at the beauty salon.

The Watkins man whisked out a bottle of shampoo and, cleverly realizing that his sale was at an end, gave Mama the bill, and she paid him. He packed up his case and left us with a cheery, "Thank you for your good order. You'll be satisfied with everything—or you let me know."

I enjoyed the Watkins man's visit as though it were a stage show.

The Rawleigh man came sometimes. Mama bought just enough from him (a few spices usually) to stay on his regular route. His visits were definitely prosaic compared to those of the Watkins man.

A FARM FIRE

We were engrossed in a chapter of the *Caddy Atkins* book Miss Shook read to us every day after lunch, when we were startled by a demanding knock on our schoolhouse door. Miss Shook dropped the book on her desk and, after a moment's hesitation, hurried to the door. She burst back into the room, looking stunned.

"My parents' house is on fire! School is dismissed. Get your wraps on and go home, or go with a friend if you mother isn't home." Her face was white and her voice shook as she supervised the children's departure.

The neighbor who had come with the news waited with his team and wagon to take Miss Shook to the home where she lived with her parents in the 1920s. Harry and I rode along as far as our house, gripping the edge of the wagon as we stood inside.

"Can they get it out? How did it start?" asked our teacher in gasping breaths.

"It looks bad," the man answered. "I came to get you as soon as I saw they had enough help. I didn't hear how it started. They have a bucket brigade going. They'll do all they can."

The horses struggled to pull the wagon as it bumped over the ruts, sinking in where the spring sun had thawed the frigid ground in this wooded area. The driver slapped the reins on the horses' backs, urging them to a trot as we drove out of the woods. Miss Shook shriveled up into her coat and sat tensely on the seat, saying no more.

Mama knew about the fire because Central had alerted people in the area with a line ring—a long ring on the party line used to give emergency information to everyone on the line.

"Can we go see it?" I asked. I had never seen a house burn. It sounded exciting.

Mama hesitated. "We don't want to get in the way. But maybe Mrs. Shook will need her friends around her. We'll go see what we can do to help."

We parked by the side of the road. A bonfire smell filled the air as we hurried into the yard. Flames were blazing out of all the upstairs windows. Men who had been ineffectually trying to put out the fire by passing water buckets from one to the other stood in the mud, watching. A knot of men who had been carrying furniture out of the house milled around, repelled by the heat. One man said, "The roof will go any time. We daren't try to save anything more."

Pieces of furniture had been hastily pulled from the house: a table and some chairs, a chest of drawers, a couch, a rug. It seemed very little to come from such a big house.

Mrs. Shook was standing by the furniture, wiping her eyes on her apron. Mama went over to say a few words of comfort to her. "I'm so sorry," she offered. "We'll all pitch in and help you get started again, with kitchen things, bedding and all. You have lots of friends who care."

"I know, I know. And I'm so thankful no one was hurt. I kept hearing a crackling noise all morning as I was baking, but I couldn't figure out what it was. I thought it must be squirrels playing on the roof. That's how it got such a start. Frank was driving by, and he noticed smoke coming out of the attic windows. Oh, Dorothy, everything is gone," and tears rolled down her cheeks again.

Just then the roof fell in, and the house collapsed into itself with a loud "whoo-oosh." A gasp went up from the watchers. We stood hushed, hardly breathing. A display of sparks flew upward like fireworks on the Fourth of July, and brands of burning wood flew everywhere. People began to leave quietly. A few men stayed to oversee the burning hulk and to see that no other buildings caught fire. The family members huddled together.

As we walked away, burning pieces of printed paper blew toward me. I turned back and saw a book afire, leaves curling and blowing away, one by one. Books, I thought! It's terrible to see books burning, something to read being wasted. Then I thought of what a fire could take away from us: our baby pictures, the little chair where Mama rocked me, the wedding gift cut glass cream and sugar set that Mama treasured. A lump filled my throat. I understood why Mrs. Shook cried. A fire wasn't an exciting spectacle. It was a tragedy.

Miss Shook told us the next day that her family was staying with her married sister and that they were grateful to the friends who had done so much to help. She had dark circles under her eyes and sat with her head in her hands, elbows on her desk, while we were studying. We pupils were considerate for the next few days, as if someone had died.

THE SUNDAY SCHOOL PICNIC

A ripple of excitement ran through the congregation one July Sunday when I was ten, when Rev. Baker announced that the Sunday School picnic would be held the following Thursday. We had been waiting for this. The picnic was an annual event, held at Round Grove, a park on the Shell Rock River a few miles upstream from Greene. It was the most popular place for picnics, with shade from several acres of oak, elm, and maple trees.

After church Mama and some of her friends gathered in a circle outside to plan what main dishes each would take to the picnic.

"I'm using new potatoes now. I'll cream some with fresh peas," Mrs. Downs began the planning.

"I've still got old potatoes, so I'll bring potato salad," Mama went on.

"My chicks will be big enough. I'll fry a couple." I was glad to hear this from Mrs. Mather, whose fried chicken was my favorite.

Aunt Jen promised her moist, tender angel food, and Mama offered her red mahogany (chocolate) cake. "And Paul will freeze ice cream."

Each woman would add her specialties to her picnic basket. Mama always bought soft sweet buns from the store and made sandwiches of boiled ham, with its rim of white fat around the edges. It was a rare treat, not served to us on ordinary days.

On picnic day we woke up to the sound of rain. "Why does it have to rain today?" I complained.

"That's what makes the corn grow in Iowa: hot days and rainy nights."

"Will it ever stop?"

Mama was cooking dressing for potato salad. The vinegar, mustard, sugar smell made my mouth water.

"Rain before seven, clear before eleven," she recited.

And with that I had to be satisfied. I fixed myself a bowl of Post Toasties with cream and sugar. Mama toasted a piece of bread for me on the stove top as she stirred the salad dressing.

"Where's Pa? Isn't he going to the picnic?"

"He and Harry have the chores to do, and they have to finish shocking the oats, wet as it is. They'll be done in plenty of time. Get me a basket of cobs. You'll feel better if you're doing something."

On my way to the cob house, I stopped to watch the rain clouds scudding across the sky. The rain was blowing over.

Papa and Harry came in from the field, washed at the kitchen sink, and put on clean clothes. I slipped into my nainsook slip and dotted Swiss dress, pulled on long cotton lisle stockings, and fastened them to my garter belt.

Finally we were on our way. Our drive to Round Grove took us past a farm with big lilac bushes in the front yard, only a mile from Round Grove. If only we lived there, I could walk to the picnic and be as early as I wanted to.

Driving between the fenced-in rows of tall corn on each side of the lane leading to the park was like going through an endless tunnel. I was in a fever of excitement. Was I missing something? Were the girls already exploring? Or had they started eating? We finally were there, and my fears were groundless. I hadn't missed a thing.

All of us helped Mama carry our food to the picnic tables in the shelter. Then Papa and Harry left to seek congenial male company. Dale raced to the slippery slide. Mama tossed an old tablecloth over a section of tables, and we straightened it, one on each side.

The shelter had a cement floor and was covered with a rustic wooden roof. A dozen tables were lined up in rows. Mama put our food on a table reserved for this use, and she set our places beside those of another family.

I watched as little Darrell came running to his mother with a bleeding finger, which he had scratched on a nail on a teeter-totter. She tore a narrow strip off a soft, clean towel and wrapped it around and around the affected finger, making a cloth thimble over the end as well. With a quick jerk she tore the end of the strip into two narrower strips, wrapped them opposite ways around the bandage, and tied a secure knot below the sore. Satisfied, the victim ran off to resume play.

Swinging around a post supporting the roof, I had been observing who was at the picnic. I edged into a group of girls who were walking around. We knew each other slightly from Sunday School. One girl, Nadine, was my friend. Not only was she my twin, but her first name was also Margaret. When we were three, we had shoes alike, black high-top button shoes with white tassels at the top. At the time, these girls went to town school while I attended a rural school. They also played together in the summertime. They accepted me at once, but for awhile I stayed on the fringes of the group, quietly observing their actions and how they talked to one another.

First we tried to peer in the windows of several closed-up cabins a short distance up the river. These little houses, like

Margaret Ott,
wearing shoes with white tassels
like Nadine's.

grown-ups' dollhouses, had fanciful names like "Florence's Folly" and "Nianza." They looked deserted, mysterious, with the blinds securely down and the doors tightly shut. I knew they belonged to members of the Round Grove Association, who spent hot days here sometimes, where the cool breezes blew in from the river.

Two of the older boys were offering rowboat rides. I was afraid to go because I couldn't swim. We talked about wading, but a man sitting on the bank said it wasn't safe to wade right here. The water, sparkling in the sun and gurgling as it swept along, did look cool and inviting on this hot day. We watched it until our eyes blurred, then regretfully walked away.

Having saved our favorite place for the last fun before dinner, we approached a trim cabin in the park near the picnic area, where some of the boys had already gathered. This was the home of a man who must have taken care of the park, although he never worked at it while we were there. He was a small, neat, sunbrowned man, wearing all brown clothing. This brownness gave him an aura of mystery, seeming to associate him with storybook characters of woodsmen or gnomes. His yard was an adventureland to us. In a cage sitting on a high table, two mice ran endlessly on a wheel. Hazel asked him how he had trained them to run so fast and so long. He replied briefly, "I didn't train them. That's a treadmill. They run because it's their nature."

While we were there, he busied himself with small chores around his yard, not seeming to watch us. He smiled slightly to himself at our enthusiasm and moved over to put another machine in motion for us to watch. It looked so simple, but we couldn't see how the stream of water in the top trough ran down at exactly the right time to fall into the next trough as it moved into place, then reversed to do it over again. He stepped protectively over to the industrious mice when Roger poked a stick at them through the cage. No words were spoken, but Roger moved back quickly from the cage.

Nailed to the tree was a small animal skull. Under it was a hand-carved sign on a board: "Alas, Poor Yorick." As with so many puzzling things in my life, I didn't ask what it meant. I was delighted to discover in college that the phrase was from Shakespeare.

We were entranced with the workings of another contraption. It had wheels, belts, levers, and balls that rolled about. One movement derived from another in a pattern we couldn't understand. When I saw a Rube Goldberg creation years later, I knew I had seen one of that ilk at Round Grove.

The women at the picnic tables called for us to line up and fill our plates. Children, so often expected to be seen and not heard, were allowed at the picnic to be first at the tables. An immense array of food was spread on the tables, on platters and dishes and in baskets. All our lives we'd been sampling food these cooks made, and so we knew what a treat we faced. Mrs. Mather's fried chicken, Mama's sandwiches and crab apple pickles, and spicy wieners were my choice. Jello salad, a luxury in hot weather, brought straight from Miss Stauffer's icebox, disappeared with the first wave of eaters. There were pies — apple, cherry, gooseberry, lemon — and an equal abundance of cakes. Who could decide? One of my favorite desserts, made of pearl tapioca boiled in water until clear, then mixed with fresh fruit and whipped cream, was heaped in a big glass bowl. The ladies waved dish towels to shoo flies away from the food, and they urged us on:

"Fill up your plates, now. Don't go away hungry." As if we could!

We had time to run around a bit and let this huge meal begin to digest while the adults ate. Then the ice cream freezers were lined up at the edges of the shelter floor. The men pulled out the corks on the side of the freezers and tipped them, letting the salt water run out. Finally they opened the freezers, and we children crowded around. I had only a small cone of Mrs. Cheney's vanilla. I liked hers because she made it without eggs and it wasn't so rich. After the games I would have Mama's chocolate. The men dishing from the freezers pretended to believe that each child was entitled to only one cone, thus adding to the fun of getting in line again to see if we would get away with it. A man might ask, severely,

Nianza Cottage.

"Didn't I see you in line before?"

The culprit would insist, "No, that was my brother."

No one was fooled by any of this. The men were as anxious as the women to please us, and they would dip as much as we asked for. Papa affected disbelief when small Ralph came up for his third cone: "You must have a hollow leg, young man!"

The men now rested and talked, or napped, not being used to so much food or leisure in the middle of the day.

The women cleared up and then sat fanning themselves, discussing ailments and homespun remedies, exchanging recipes and household hints. Babies were passed around, giving their young mothers a few moments of respite. Mothers whose children were grown held out welcoming arms to fussy toddlers fighting sleep, cuddling and humming them to a state of relaxation.

We girls, a tightly knit group now, took time out to go to the restroom. The outdoor toilet was just like ours at home except that this one had real toilet paper. Shocked, I read my first graffiti, this day, on the inside wall of that building. The jingle is etched on my brain, though I had to guess at its meaning then.

We headed over the gravelly grass to the slides, swings, and seesaws. A group of boys drifted our way. A boy named Lyle walked up on one side of a seesaw, balanced daringly at the top until the other end hit the ground, then ran down it. Glenn was pumping a swing as high as it would go. We watched these feats out of the corners of our eyes. Ralph teased me.

"Margaret likes Dale S. Come on, Dale, give her a hug."

Scarlet with embarrassment, I climbed up the chute of the slide to hide my face. We girls loved the teasing, expected it, had come over here for it, but we would have died rather than to admit such a thing.

Just as we tired of this sport, the call came for the organized games. These games took place on the smooth green grass of the golf course, which was usually off limits to us: leapfrog, sack races, three-legged races, and distance races for all age groups. Nadine and I won second place in the three-legged race. Those in charge were careful to have enough categories so that even the smallest and slowest contestant won a prize, an all-day sucker.

After this, some of the more agile men played a not-so-lively game of softball, with plenty of joshing by both teams. I didn't find this interesting, and they didn't seem enthusiastic either.

"Anyone want ice cream?" called one of the bystanders, and the game was abandoned. Several boys rushed to the freezers. There was plenty left. Now came the boys' last chance to see how many cones they could eat. The men who were dishing were glad enough to get rid of the softening ice cream.

Waiting in line for my chocolate cone, I heard an older boy say, "I've had five and I'm going after another one."

It looked cloudy again, and the men watched the sky.

"Mama, is it going to rain?" I asked.

"Not if there's enough blue sky to make a Dutchman a pair of britches," she answered.

"How big a Dutchman would that be, Dorothy?" asked Genie, with a twinkle in her eye.

Women put picnic baskets back into the cars and rounded up tired children.

"We have to get home. Percy has hay down," said Helen, and the family left, soon followed by others.

"Goodbye," we called as we left.

A WOMAN'S-EYE VIEW OF THRESHING

After dinner Mama threw the dishwater over the fence and sat on the edge of a chair to read the paper. It slipped to the table as she stared into space. She jumped up, took eggs and flour, and began to make noodles. The phone rang.

"Dorothy, they'll finish here about five o'clock, so they'll be at your place tomorrow. John says he'll get the rig moved tonight."

"I've been half planning on them. What did you serve today?" We'd be feeding twenty-five to thirty hungry threshers for dinner and supper tomorrow and the next day. Mama didn't want to duplicate the meat the men had just been served. She seemed to believe that her reputation as a cook depended on serving excellent meals for the threshers. It was a challenge to be met, and she expressed her satisfaction when Papa compared her meals favorably with others served on the ring.

In 1929 Papa belonged to a threshing ring of ten to twelve farmers. The group hired a man with a modern gas threshing machine, although a few old coal burners were still around, spewing out their greasy, dirty smoke. The men went from farm to farm, each helping the others with the big task of "thrashing." Some men hired extra help, and the boys in the families did their part.

Although the order of going from farm to farm was planned, a heavy rain had caused a slowdown. The women kept each other apprised of developments and made plans to exchange help on threshing days. Three women usually worked together, with the extra help of young girls in the family. My friend, Deon Ramker, came to work with me and to flirt with the boys, and I went to her house for the same reasons. Her mother would have the crew next.

Mama was up by five o'clock the next morning, baking pies — three apple, two rhubarb — and three crusts to be filled later. She called in her order to the grocer: an eight-pound beef roast, ground meat, cold cuts, lemons, and bread. She made a quick trip into town to pick it up, leaving ten-month-old Dean in my care.

Zula called at eight-thirty: "How's it going, Dorothy? Do you need me for anything right now? Or Deon could come any time if that would help."

"I've got my pies done and have been to town for my groceries. The roast is in the oven. I'll be all right for another hour or so. I'm usually pretty well organized the first day."

Mama had killed and plucked two hens. To singe them, she took a round lid off the stove, wadded up a piece of newspaper, caught it afire on one side, and, with the skill of long practice, pulled the flaming paper out of the fire with one hand and swished it over the chicken held up in the other. The burning hair smell of pin feathers quickly blended into the amalgam of meat, coffee, apple pie, and wood fire smells.

She soon had the hens cut up and boiling for her rich chicken and noodles. Yesterday she had made the noodles, thick and chewy.

"Margaret, run out and pick tomatoes for me. I'll need a couple of heads of cabbage, too. When that's done, get the wash dishes and towels out for the men."

I set two wash basins on old backless chairs out by the well and clothes-pinned several roller linen towels to the adjacent clothesline. I filled a laundry tub with well water, to let it warm in the sun, and hung the dipper on the side of the tub. Soap was nearby on an old saucer. I hung a mirror on the windmill, put out a comb, and propped up a broom so the men could sweep straw off their overalls, especially the men who were stacking the straw pile.

A stacker with a pitchfork worked at each end of the stack growing under his feet as the blower spouting straw moved back and forth in a slight arc. The stacker waded in the new straw and forked it evenly on his half of the stack, interlocking the straw so it was bound together tightly and smoothly. A good stack would not be blown away by the wind, nor would it collapse if cattle nibbled a cave-like opening at the bottom. The man had only the time the blower deposited straw on the other half of the stack to accomplish this. Each farmer picked his own stackers. Though it was hard, dirty work, it was an honor to be asked. Each brought his own fork, wore bandannas tied over his nose and mouth, and had his shirt and overalls fastened tightly at wrist and ankles with wide rubber bands cut from inner tubes. Pa raised a little barley, so the stackers complained good-naturedly about getting the prickly barley beards under their clothes.

The women set about their work with few words. Mrs. Johnson peeled a huge kettle of potatoes and took charge of mashing them with cream, adding big chunks of butter on top of the white mounds in the serving dishes. Zula dipped fully ripe tomatoes in scalding water to loosen the skins, then peeled and sliced them. Mama shredded cabbage and onions, mixed it with celery seed, salt, and a dressing she mixed up with sour cream, sugar, and vinegar.

When Mama told me they were through using the kitchen table for a work surface, Deon and I stretched its ends apart and inserted all its leaves. With one of us at each end, we spread it with Mama's white linen tablecloth and set it, making sure there was a chair for each place setting. As food was prepared, we put it on tables set up on the front porch and in the back kitchen.

When extended, the table reached very near to the stove, which felt hot as the sun while the mountains of food cooked. We were inured to the heat, and the adrenaline was flowing. We had never heard of air-conditioning in a home.

"Dale, you and Jerry (Deon's younger brother) stop running in and out. You'll let in every fly in the neighborhood. If you don't know what to do with yourselves, take a towel and see if you can swish some of the pesky things away from that screen door," Mama advised.

Deon and I kept swatting the flies and chasing them away from the food. It was a losing battle, but we were used to that, too.

It was our job to dish pickles, applesauce, jelly, and cucumbers, and to be sure cream and sugar, as well as bread and butter, were placed at each end of the table. Mama had her good Burns' bread knife, which made slicing bread easy.

Our threshing ring shared a big coffee pot, which made the rounds. I asked Papa why he drank hot coffee when he was already so hot. "It keeps me cool," he said. He had given me the same answer once before when I asked why he wore long-legged underwear all summer. I thought he was teasing me. Eventually I learned about the cooling power of evaporation.

The men came in to eat as their hayrack loads of bundles were deposited into the machine, instead of the whole crew at once, so the table space and the available chairs worked out all right. Some of them hesitated to sit down at the white tablecloth, saying they hated to dirty it. Mama told them, "Don't you worry about that. As hard as you men work, I want you to have the best." Several years later she did buy a long piece of white oilcloth, rolling it on its cardboard cylinder and storing it in the seedcorn room between threshings.

Deon and I were expected to save our nonsense until later and instead watched the table, refilling bowls and glasses as needed. The men swilled down water and lemonade to make up for dripping sweat during their hours of work in the sun. It made me feel grown up to do such necessary tasks.

Tired of entertaining the men from his highchair, Dean began to fuss. I slung him up to my hip and went on pouring water with my right hand. Soon he sagged against me, sound asleep, so I laid him down in his crib.

Zula kept washing plates, glasses, and silverware to reset the places. None of the men sat down to rest after eating. They wanted to keep on with the work and get it done.

After the women had eaten and had washed and rinsed the dishes in two big dishpans on the cool end of the stove, they had a little break in the afternoon to sit and fan themselves. Mrs. Johnson said, "I'm sure glad our ring doesn't expect lunches in the morning and afternoon." Some of the German farmers had this custom.

Sociability was a benefit of the women's getting together. They did a lot of downright hard work, but it was done in a spirit of camaraderie. As they rested, Mrs. Johnson talked about the problems her daughter was having with her pregnancy, and the others filled in with opinions and advice. Zula brought up the concerns she and Louis had about starting a dairy. Deon and I were all ears, though we pretended to carry on our own conversation. We heard little tidbits to speculate about later.

Because we had no refrigeration or icebox, all the food preparation had to be accomplished just before the meal at which it was to be served. Most leftovers were tossed over the fence to the chickens. Our cooling device was a wooden tank in the milk house near the well. Water, hand-numbing cold, ran into the tank almost constantly in hot weather. A gasoline pump, chug-chugging and backfiring, drew up water when there was not enough wind to turn the big wheel on top of the windmill. Fruit jars of milk and cream, and butter and other foods in pans, fit into square compartments along the back wall of the tank and kept reasonably cold. The tank's capacity was limited by the tall cans of cream cooling after going through the separator. When I lifted up the cover of the tank on a hot day and bent over to lift out a jar of milk, I inhaled a cool mist of milky-smelling vapor arising from the tank. Water from this tank was gravity-fed to the stock tank in the barnyard.

Mama listened as the women talked, but she kept on working, although at a more leisurely pace than in the morning, starting to get ready another heavy meal for supper. She mixed ground beef and ham with onions, crackers, and tomato juice for a meat loaf. Instead of a second hot meat as she had served at noon, she would put out cold cuts and wedges sliced from a big wheel of Longhorn cheese. Cake had been served at noon, so the pies were cut for supper, along with leftover cake.

To make a filling for the piecrusts, I mixed sugar, cornstarch and cocoa together, then stirred it slowly into cold milk in a pan. I heated this on the stove until it boiled. I separated eggs, beat the yolks with a fork, then put a few spoonsful of the hot mixture into the yolks, stirred well before adding it to the filling in the pan, and cooked it until it was thick. Finally, I poured it into the crusts. Then I made a meringue, beating the egg whites and a little sugar with the egg beater. When it was stiff, I swirled it over the pies and slid them into the oven to brown the meringue. Mama watched them for me, taking them out as she put in the meat loaf.

Supper was a more relaxed meal, and we girls had more time to flirt with the boys. We teased them about the amount of food they ate, and they lived up to our expectations. "Peaches" was the big eater in our ring. When it came to number of pieces of pie consumed at one meal, he was the undisputed champion. He usually ate four, if there was plenty of pie, but if challenged, he could do better.

The next morning it rained again, stopping the work for a few hours. Pa had estimated we'd be done by noon and the rig would move on right after dinner. Because of the rain the men would be at our place for supper.

Mama called Zula. "The rain slowed the men down. They'll be here for supper. You can take your beauty nap this afternoon."

"I'll bring you my pies, then, and I have fryers dressed. That will be a start for you."

"I'll get something together for the rest of the meal. Ellen will stay on and help. I'll bake for you in the morning."

Threshing accomplished, farm people had a breather before the next big task, picking corn. It was even possible to take a vacation, if Papa could get someone to do the chores.

Epilogue

From the fabric of my earliest life, I have pulled a few threads of memory. The love and security of my family has followed like a golden thread through the ensuing years, making it possible for me to achieve one goal after another. The wistful little girl, who felt she was on the outside looking in, grew ever so slowly into a self-confident woman. Though I often seemed to be a step behind my contemporaries, it was all worth waiting for.

The first goal was realized in 1940, when I graduated from Cornell College with a major in home economics. After four years of teaching, I married a fellow teacher who was by then in the United States Army.

After the war my husband resumed teaching instrumental music, and I stayed home and had babies, five in all. Our children were, and are, the joy of our lives. Life had given me what I had most wanted.

Gradually, a new goal became uppermost in my mind, that all five of our children should graduate from college. One teacher's salary seemed to be inadequate for such an undertaking.

When our youngest child started school, I began teaching homemaking in a junior high school. It was a busy life. The whole family worked together to make it possible. I especially enjoyed teaching sewing, and I sewed compulsively at home as well. To have a successful career was fulfilling to me.

I thank our children for grasping my dream and making it come true. After the fifth had graduated, I put down my needle and took up my pen. A new goal has now been achieved with the publication of this book.

All of life's experiences teach us something of value. Waiting and wanting develop character. Things longed for and worked for are all the more precious when received, be they club memberships or tangible objects. Every child should have the privilege of occasionally being denied instant gratification of some wish or whim.

And still the loom weaves on.

> Grow old along with me!
> The best is yet to be,
> The last of life for which the first was made. . . .

— Rabbi ben Ezra (Browning)